Designing
Engineering
Solutions

Inventors of Food and Agriculture Technology

Heather S. Morrison

Cavendish
Square

New York

Published in 2016 by Cavendish Square Publishing, LLC
243 5th Avenue, Suite 136, New York, NY 10016

Copyright © 2016 by Cavendish Square Publishing, LLC

First Edition

Cataloging-in-Publication Data

Morrison, Heather S.
Inventors of food and agriculture technology / by Heather S. Morrison.
p. cm. — (Designing engineering solutions)
Includes index.
ISBN 978-1-50260-664-8 (hardcover) ISBN 978-1-50260-665-5 (ebook)
1. Sustainable agriculture — Juvenile literature. 2. Food supply — Juvenile literature.
3. Inventors — Biography — Juvenile literature. I. Morrison, Heather S. II. Title.
S519.M67 2016
630—d23

The author would like to thank the following contributors: Laura Lambert,
Paul Schellinger, Mary Sisson, Cathleen Small, Chris Woodford

Editorial Director: David McNamara
Editor: Kristen Susienka
Copy Editor: Michele Suchomel-Casey
Art Director: Jeffrey Talbot
Designer: Alan Sliwinski
Senior Production Manager: Jennifer Ryder-Talbot
Production Editor: Renni Johnson
Photo Research: J8 Media

Printed in the United States of America

Contents

Introduction to Food and Agriculture Technology

For over two millennia humanity has depended on food grown on the land for survival. Today, many people get the food they eat from grocery stores or local markets, but those places still receive food they sell from farmers across the country and around the world. Without advancements in food processing and agricultural techniques, the world's population—now the largest in history— would be much lower than it currently is, and more people would be without food. Still, there is concern that some modern methods of food production are not the safest and could lead to harmful chronic illnesses such as obesity and certain types of cancer. Moreover, controversy remains that even though there is an abundance of food in certain parts of the world, many thousands of people still suffer. Whether or not today's scientists and leading inventors in these industries will work to solve these problems is unknown; however, there have been many innovative techniques and improvements that give hope for the future.

The History of Agriculture

Agriculture began in the Middle East approximately ten thousand to eleven thousand years ago. Before this time, most people lived as **hunter-gatherers**, getting their food whenever they needed to, much as animals do, by hunting and fishing or gathering wild plants. Agriculture offered a more systematic way of producing the food people needed to survive. Societies gradually began to **domesticate** animals, plant crops, and develop better tools. These tools included picks; digging sticks for sowing seeds, cultivation, and harvest; and plows, specifically to help them farm the land. Many basic farming techniques developed in this time are still used. For example, hillsides were first terraced (cut into steps to make level growing areas) in Peru and other countries thousands of years ago, whereas farmers were making attempts to select plants that could resist diseases about nine thousand years ago.

Plants need huge amounts of water, so in arid areas like the Middle East moving water from lowland rivers to crops on higher ground was a major endeavor. Some of the earliest Middle Eastern inventions are devices for raising and moving water, developed in ancient times. Around 1400 BCE, the ancient Egyptians invented a type of water crane known as a *shadoof*. Working in a manner similar to a seesaw, it had a bucket at one end and a heavy weight at the other. Using a series of shadoofs, Egyptians could raise water through all the levels of a terrace. A more efficient water-raising device was invented by ancient Greek engineer and mathematician Archimedes (ca. 287–212 BCE). The device was a giant screw that drew water up a hollow pipe when the operator cranked a handle. The Roman Empire (27 BCE–395 CE) introduced Middle Eastern farming techniques to Europe and pioneered irrigation canals and aqueducts for carrying water to farms.

The Importance of Harnesses

Some of the simplest agricultural inventions have had the greatest impact. When horses were used as work animals in ancient times, loads were attached to straps around their necks. During the Middle Ages (the period from the fall of the Roman Empire to about the fifteenth century), European farmers began using harnesses that distributed the load more evenly around the animal's body. This simple improvement enabled the horse to breathe more easily and work harder. Eventually, harnessed horses could pull a plow several times faster than an ox. Such harnesses greatly increased productivity and helped to make individual farmers more wealthy and independent.

Toward the end of the Middle Ages, explorers set off on great ocean voyages to conquer the world. In the Americas, explorers were surprised to find Native Americans already using advanced agricultural techniques, and the Europeans took the foods they discovered back to their homelands. In this way, European countries learned of foods and other goods such as chocolate, corn (maize), potatoes, rubber, tobacco, and tomatoes from the Americas, and coffee and tea from Asia.

The Age of Machines

A new phase in the history of agriculture began in Britain around 1700 and spread throughout Europe and North America during the next two centuries. Better ways of growing crops and improved methods of breeding livestock were two of the forces behind the agricultural revolution, as this period became known. The third major force was an improvement in farm machinery. One of the pioneers of mechanized farming was English farmer Jethro Tull (1674–1741), who developed an improved drill for pushing seeds into the ground in 1701. Tull's invention made the sowing of seed more efficient, thus reducing the amount of seed needed to achieve the same acreage of crop. He also developed a hoe drawn by horses that ripped up weeds and **aerated** the soil as it was pulled through the fields.

Tull had not invented the idea of drilling seeds—which dates from ancient times—but he used technology to do the same job more quickly and efficiently. John Deere (1804–1886), a blacksmith from

This photograph shows farmers on a North American prairie harvesting their land in the late nineteenth or early twentieth century.

Illinois, was another inventor who refined existing technology. In 1837, he invented a new form of plow made from highly polished steel: a toughened form of iron popularized by Henry Bessemer (1813–1898). It was more effective at moving through heavy soil than earlier plows made from iron and wood, and it played an important role in the expansion of agriculture in the Midwest.

Machines were also invented for the harvesting of crops. One of the pioneers was Cyrus Hall McCormick (1809–1884), who developed a horse-drawn reaping machine in 1831 for cutting grain. Later that decade, the brothers John and Hiram Pitts of Winthrop, Maine, patented the first **thresher**. Combine harvesters were also invented in the nineteenth century. As their name suggests, they worked by combining reaping and threshing in a single machine. However, they were not widely used for many decades.

Agriculture Advances

All these early machines were horse-powered, but several new ways of driving farm machines emerged after the mid-nineteenth century. Steam power was pioneered by English blacksmith Thomas Newcomen (1663–1729), who built his first, huge steam engine for pumping wastewater out of a deep coal mine in 1712. Smaller steam engines were later used in railroad locomotives and ships. By the mid-nineteenth century, inventors were using stationary steam engines on farms, mainly to drive threshing machines. Traction engines (large tractors powered by steam) became popular in the decades that followed.

Steam engines were cumbersome and inefficient, but better power sources soon appeared. German inventor Nikolaus August Otto (1832–1891) invented the gasoline engine in 1867, and his compatriot Rudolf Diesel (1858–1913) developed his doubly efficient diesel engine in the 1890s. Gas and diesel engines, also known as internal combustion engines, played an important part in the continuing agricultural revolution as they came to be used in cars, trucks, and tractors. Automobile pioneer Henry Ford (1863–1947), who was raised on a farm, helped many more farmers to afford tractors when he introduced his inexpensive Fordson Model F in 1917. Aircraft also played a part in modern agriculture, aiding activities such as crop dusting. They were developed after American brothers Orville (1871–1948) and Wilbur Wright (1867–1912) mounted a gasoline engine on a glider to make the first powered flight in 1903.

During the twentieth century, electricity became increasingly important in powering farm machines. Electric power became available during the 1880s when the American inventor Thomas Edison (1847–1931) built his first power plant in New York City. Most farms in Europe and the United States were using electric power by the end of the 1930s.

Spending on Disposable Income

According to the US Department of Agriculture, in 2013, Americans spent 5.6 percent of their disposable income on food bought for the home and 4.3 percent on food away from home. Those numbers are down from what they were a few years ago and certainly much lower than what they were decades before. As disposable income climbs, the percentage spent on food drops: in 1970, Americans spent 13.9 percent of their disposable income on food; in 1950, 20.6 percent.

Land and Crop Developments

No amount of machinery can force crops from poor land, so the development of scientific methods of farming in the nineteenth century was just as important as the arrival of engines, tractors, and electricity. A pioneer in this field was the English chemist Humphry Davy (1778–1829), who explained his ideas on using chemicals to fertilize plants in 1813. Three decades later, in 1842, English scientist John Bennet Lawes (1814–1900) patented a way of fertilizing crops with phosphates, the basis for the huge industry that grew up to develop and provide artificial fertilizers.

Another form of treating land chemically, using pesticides to kill insects, became possible with the discovery of dichlorodiphenyl-trichloroethane (DDT), a chemical originally developed to kill mosquitoes. In 1942, Swiss chemist Paul Müller (1899–1965) found that DDT was an effective way of killing a wide variety of agricultural pests, such as the louse and the Colorado beetle. A whole series of similar pesticides were developed from DDT in the years that followed. Initially, such chemicals seemed to offer a cure-all: they killed pests, prevented the spread of diseases such as typhoid and malaria, and saved crops and lives. However, in the 1950s and 1960s, these chemicals were found to be immensely toxic and very persistent in the environment and in the bodies of animals and humans. Some, including DDT, were later banned in the United States and other parts of the world.

Botany began in ancient times when the Romans were the first to breed plants selectively by carefully picking the best examples and cultivating them. Only in the nineteenth century, however, did selective plant breeding begin to develop into a truly systematic science. Agricultural scientists at this time raised plants in laboratories and carried out experiments to develop better varieties (slightly different versions of the same plant species). Luther Burbank (1849–1926), for example, developed improved varieties of many plants, including potatoes, plums, roses, corn, and tomatoes, and in 1921, he set out his ideas in a book called *How Plants Are Trained to Work for Man*. Burbank's title could have been a personal motto for the life of George Washington Carver (1864–1943), an African-American inventor who developed hundreds of useful products from peanuts and sweet potatoes.

Developing improved varieties of crops has also played a crucial role in the battle to feed the world. In the mid-twentieth century, US agricultural scientist Norman Borlaug (1914–2009) developed new varieties of wheat and other grains that were more resistant to disease and produced far higher yields. Borlaug's work contributed to saving hundreds of millions of people in developing countries from starvation and earned him the Nobel Peace Prize in 1970. Such advances became known as the "**green** revolution," the idea that agricultural innovations could solve the problem of world hunger.

Food Consumption and Preservation

Produce often endures long periods between leaving the farm and arriving in grocery stores or homes. As transporting food grown in distant places has become easier, preserving food has become

Food for the Future

Making enough food for an increasing population has often involved controversial practices, although people have not always seen them as such. Slave labor, for example, was normal in ancient Rome, where slaves ran the huge farms that fed the Roman Empire and even powered many of its machines by walking endlessly on or inside treadmills. Slavery was not widely considered unacceptable until the nineteenth century, when Africans were being imported into the southern United States by the tens of thousands to enable the growth of the cotton industry.

Sometimes the controversial aspects of new technologies are not immediately apparent. Chemical pesticides (insect killers) and herbicides (weed killers) seemed to offer farmers a miraculous way of increasing crop yields when they first appeared during World War II. Then, in 1962, ecologist Rachel Carson (1907–1964) published a damning book, *Silent Spring*, that documented what she saw as the dangers to plants, animals, and humans. Passionately opposed to the new technology, she argued, "Chemicals are the increasingly crucial. Most of the foods people eat in Western countries are preserved in some way.

A French chef, Nicolas-François Appert (ca. 1750–1841), was one of the first inventors to tackle food preservation. In 1810, he invented a way of heating and canning food to keep it safe to eat for longer periods. This technique made possible the development of industrial canning during the nineteenth century. Inventors such as Appert knew how to preserve food but not why it spoiled or how their methods worked. Answers to those questions also came from France. Louis Pasteur (1822–1895), a French chemist and biologist, discovered that food spoils because of bacteria growing inside it. He developed a method of heating food, called pasteurization, that kills bacteria and makes food safe for longer periods of time. An alternative means to the same end is to cool food so that the bacteria grow more slowly. In the 1920s, American inventor Clarence Birdseye (1886–1956) perfected a way of quickly freezing foods such as fish so

sinister and little-recognized partners of radiation in changing the very nature of the world—the very nature of its life."

Developments in **biotechnology** since the 1970s have caused a whole new series of controversies. Some scientists believe **genetically modified organisms** (also known as GMOs or **transgenic** organisms) offer the best hope of feeding the earth's growing population. Yet many environmentalists fear that GM technology could contaminate natural plants, produce "super-pests" that cannot be controlled, and have other unforeseen consequences. Today there have been significant improvements and increased use of GMOs, but concerns of the consequences of their continued use remain.

Sometimes fears of the future are justified. In 1800, around 90 percent of the US population worked in agriculture, whereas now that figure is less than 2 percent—so it is certainly true that technology has eliminated millions of agricultural jobs. Some would see this as the price of progress. The question is not whether technology is good or bad, but whether the benefits of technology outweigh its costs—to people's lives and to the environment.

they could be kept fresh longer. Canning, pasteurization, and freezing are still the most important methods of preserving food, along with newer and more controversial technologies such as irradiation (using radioactivity to kill pests and bacteria).

Inventors have found many other ways of satisfying consumers' demand for delicious, different, and out-of-season foods. Modern breakfast cereals were invented in 1894 when Will K. Kellogg (1860–1951) and his brother John (1852–1943) forced boiled wheat through rollers and accidentally discovered corn flakes. The use of Coca-Cola, invented in the 1880s by John Pemberton (1831–1888), as a soft drink was also accidental. Originally designed as a medicinal drink, Coca-Cola was soon being bought solely because people liked its taste. Another important way to preserve foods is simply to make it easier and more convenient for people to shop for them. Clarence Saunders (1881–1953) devoted his life to developing self-service stores. His Piggly Wiggly chain, founded in 1916, effectively launched the idea of the modern supermarket. Such stores have had a dramatic impact on farming. By buying in large quantities, chain stores have made importing food from all over the world economically feasible. Whereas grocery stores would once have stocked only foods grown during a particular season, now they can sell virtually any food all year round.

Farming Today

Science and technology have brought great advances in agriculture and food production. Engineering has developed better engines and machines, agricultural science has given farmers more productive fields, and chemistry has helped to conquer pests and weeds. All these trends will continue, but biotechnology is likely to be the most important source of new breakthroughs. Biotechnology encompasses everything from brewing and making bread to cloning animals and genetically modifying crops.

Cloning, invented in the early 1970s by American scientists Herbert Boyer (1936–) and Stanley Cohen (1935–), involves manipulating **DNA** to make identical copies of an organism. Originally used to manufacture drugs like insulin (a treatment for diabetes), cloning has recently been applied to make genetically identical "copies" of farm animals. Dolly the sheep, the world's first cloned animal, was born in Scotland in 1996. Named for the singer Dolly Parton, she was created by a team of biologists led by Englishmen Keith Campbell (1954–2012) and Ian Wilmut (1944–).

A closely related technology, genetic modification, first came into widespread use in the 1990s. It involves altering the DNA of a plant or animal to give the organism some added benefit. For example, one of the first genetically modified (GM) products, a tomato dubbed "Flavr Savr," introduced in 1994, was engineered to ripen more slowly and last longer in stores. Today, other products are being genetically modified, such as mosquitoes and rice, to help eliminate or prevent certain diseases. Techniques such as GM foods and cloning have proved intensely controversial. Yet, if the ethical issues can be settled, they may offer a way of delivering more and better farm products for the earth's ever-growing population—and a way of continuing the agricultural revolution long into the future. Without people working together to tackle issues of controversy and create new methods and products that promote overall longevity, the world could encounter difficulties that harm it even further.

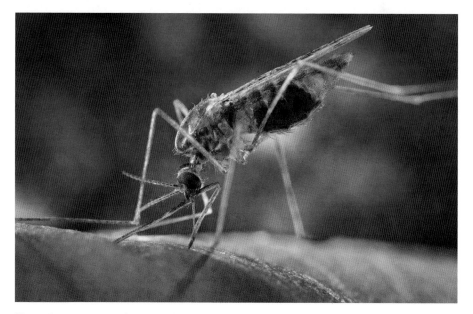

Mosquitoes are one of many animals and plants being genetically modified today.

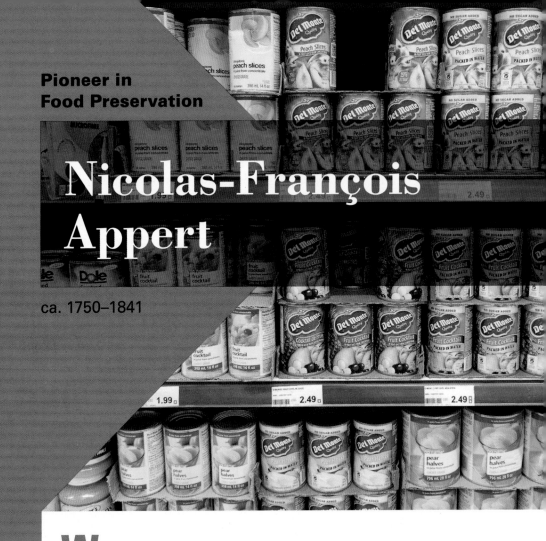

Pioneer in Food Preservation

Nicolas-François Appert

ca. 1750–1841

When you visit a supermarket, many items you pick up may come from cans, bottles, or jars. These products have gone through processes that have made them able to remain good in their containers for a longer period of time without spoiling. However, this method of preservation was not known or practiced until the nineteenth century. A man named Nicolas-François Appert developed methods of preserving food in cans or bottles, techniques still used today. It is because of him that many of our foods are stored this way.

An Inventor Begins

Appert was born around 1750 at his family's inn at Châlons-sur-Marne, France. He came from a long line of farmers and innkeepers. Although he had no formal education, he acquired many skills that would prepare him for the inventions he would make as an adult. As a child, he showed interest in food preparation and preservation; he brewed beer and pickled various foodstuffs that grew on his family's land, and he became an accomplished cook at an early age.

After serving an apprenticeship as chef at the Palais Royal Hotel in Châlons-sur-Marne, Appert left for Paris in 1780. There his talents as a confectioner became widely known, and Parisians sought him out for the pastries and other delicacies he created.

Defining the Problem

Appert opened his own candy and grocery shop in 1784. Through the 1790s, his success as a Paris grocer increased. His business grew from a small grocery to a sizable wholesale produce operation. During this period he started his experiments in various methods of preserving food. Appert deplored the primitive means of preservation used in Paris storehouses and restaurants. Up to that time, the only way of preserving food for consumption after the harvest season had ended was to process it with salt, sugar, or vinegar. These **additives**, Appert felt, compromised the nutritional value of the foods. They also diminished the taste of fresh meats and produce. Appert knew of the work that Lazzaro Spallanzani (1729–1799), an Italian biologist, had done to keep gravy fresh: he boiled it and then sealed it in a glass container. Spallanzani had also carried out the first known attempt to conserve food by heat sterilization when he boiled peas for forty-five minutes before sealing them, along with water, in a glass jar. Food processed in this manner, however, did not last long before spoiling. Appert determined to expand on Spallanzani's experiments. His key idea was that heating not only the prepared food but also the glass jar containing the food would succeed in preserving the contents indefinitely.

A desire to improve the taste and nutritional value of preserved foods was not Appert's only motivation. He was also concentrating

This illustration depicts Nicolas-François Appert.

Inventors of Food and Agriculture Technology

on the ability to transport foods. In fact, nothing less than Napoleon Bonaparte's determination to conquer the world motivated Appert to perfect his preservation methods.

Foods preserved by salting, smoking, or using additives could not be easily transported. Clearly French soldiers could not accomplish Napoleon's bold aims without being able to transport various foods that would not spoil over long distances and for extended periods. In 1795, with Napoleon preparing for his military campaign in Russia, the French government decided to offer a prize of 12,000 francs to the person who invented a method of preserving foods for its army. Appert was determined to win this prize.

Designing the Solution

In the early 1800s, he established an operation in Massy, La Maison d'Appert (House of Appert), devoted to food preservation. By 1804, this operation was functioning as a full-scale canning plant, the first in the world. It included a farm so that food could be preserved at

Louis Pasteur

the same location in which it was grown. Various kitchens were devoted to preparing meats, dairy products, and fruits and vegetables separately. In addition, separate rooms were allocated for cleaning the glass jars, labeling and packaging them, and testing new products.

With no formal education, Appert relied on his instincts and endless determination through years of trial and error. At first he used champagne bottles because they were thick enough to endure pressurization. He switched to wide-mouthed jars once these became available a few years later. Appert would fill containers with cooked food and leave room at the top to accommodate the food and liquids once they expanded. He would then cork the containers and wire down the corks before immersing the containers in boiling water. After boiling the container and its contents for a prescribed period (the time varied depending on the food), he then reinforced the cork with sealing wax to ensure longer preservation. Although he could not explain the underlying reasons for the success of the process, he observed that heating affected the fermentation of food substances. Not until some fifty years later did Louis Pasteur demonstrate the relationship between microorganisms and food spoilage.

Applying the Solution

As his packaged foods became more widely distributed, Appert's reputation also spread. In 1806, the French navy took foods packaged by Appert's Massy plant on long sea voyages. The meats, vegetables, fruits, and milk remained unspoiled more than a year later. In January 1809, after fourteen years of experimentation, Appert finally felt ready to present his products to the authorities who had offered the prize in 1795. He was awarded the 12,000 francs. The journal *Courier de l'Europe* proclaimed in February 1809 that Appert had succeeded in "making the seasons stand still." As a condition of paying Appert the 12,000 francs, the French government insisted that he publish an account of his process for the general benefit of human health and nutrition around the world. In 1810, Appert did publish a book, *The Art of Preserving All Kinds of Animal and Vegetable Substances for Several Years*, which was translated into English and published in New York two years later.

Appert enjoyed considerable fame and success in the years after 1809. Other inventors, notably Englishman Peter Durand, expanded upon Appert's method, using tin cans to package food beginning in 1810. Appert soon thereafter adopted tin as preferable to glass because glass jars would often break in transit. Despite his success, Appert always struggled financially. A cost-effective way to carry out his process was not developed until decades later. In 1814, just as his financial situation began to improve, the Prussian and Austrian armies invaded France, destroying Appert's Massy operation. He reestablished the plant at Massy after the Napoleonic Wars ended.

Along with his method for preserving food by immersing containers of cooked foods into boiling water, Appert is credited with inventing some of the objects associated with that technique. He developed an improved version of an autoclave for use as a kind of pressure cooker.

He also invented a process for making gelatin by extracting marrow, a substance in animal bones, without using acid. Appert also invented the bouillon cube, a dried, concentrated form of broth that could be rehydrated to make a soup base.

Appert died, alone and in poverty, in 1841 at age ninety-one. He was buried in a common grave. The House of Appert continued to operate in Massy until 1933.

Appertization versus Pasteurization

The process of appertization should be distinguished from the process of pasteurization that was the result of the research of the French chemist Louis Pasteur. Pasteur devised a method that could safely prepare food for storage using a much lower temperature, thereby further retaining the taste and nutrients of the food. Pasteurization is perhaps best known in connection with dairy products, which can be processed for longer, safer shelf life using Pasteur's method of low-level heating. For his part, Pasteur claimed that Appert was the first to understand the basic principle of pasteurization.

The Impact of the Solution on Society

Appert's method of preserving food, which has often been referred to as appertization, changed forever the way people thought about food. Before Appert, people had no means of keeping food in their homes for very long before it spoiled. Thus, having enough healthy food throughout the winter was difficult for many people.

By the end of the twentieth century, canned goods made up about 12 percent of grocery sales in the United States. Today, hundreds of different foods are canned, including many, such as some tropical fruits, that cannot be shipped in their fresh form to many parts of the world.

Appert was one of the first people to develop a reliable method for preserving food in cans, jars, or bottles. The concepts he introduced to the world have remained relatively unchanged today. Many people consider Appert an innovative individual who invented a system that worked and keeps on working. His legacy continues.

Timeline

ca. 1750
Nicolas-François Appert born in Châlons-sur-Marne, France

1780
Appert moves to Paris

1784
Appert opens his first grocery shop in Paris

1804
Appert opens the world's first canning plant, La Maison d'Appert, in Massy

1806
The French navy takes food packaged by Appert on long sea voyages

1809
Appert is awarded 12,000 francs by the French government for his achievements in food preservation

1810
Appert publishes a book on the art of food preservation

1814
La Maison d'Appert closes because of the invasion of France

1841
Appert dies

Clarence Birdseye

1886–1956

The food preservation industry has seen many notable people during its history. Moreover, there have been many different techniques used in the frozen food industry that have helped preserve food for longer amounts of time. One of the most well-known names in frozen foods was Clarence Birdseye. While he did not invent the modern food-freezing process, he did master the technique and has had significant influence on frozen food processes since.

Early Life

Birdseye was born in Brooklyn, New York, on December 9, 1886. One of Frank Birdseye and Ada Underwood's eight children,

Clarence spent the summers with his family on a farm on Long Island. There he cultivated a lifelong fascination with the outdoors, particularly plants and animals. As early as age ten, Birdseye was trapping and selling small animals to the Bronx Zoo to be used as food. He also studied **taxidermy** as a youth—this is worth noting,

Clarence Birdseye

given that later in life he would perfect another form of preserving organic materials.

The Birdseye family moved to Montclair, New Jersey, while Clarence was still a youth. He attended high school there and became interested in food preparation. After graduating in 1908, he attended Amherst College in Massachusetts, where he majored in biology. Birdseye quickly earned a reputation as a naturalist and as a clever entrepreneur. With his family struggling financially, Birdseye needed to support himself while in college. He continued catching and selling frogs to the Bronx Zoo to be used as reptile food, and he also caught specimens of a type of rodent for use by a Columbia University geneticist. After only two years, Birdseye left Amherst when financial pressures forced him to seek full-time work.

Birdseye took a position as a naturalist with the US Department of Agriculture's Biological Survey. He was sent first to the Southwest to collect animal and bird specimens. He continued to work on the Biological Survey during the summers of 1911 and 1912. His final summer with the survey was spent studying Rocky Mountain spotted fever in Montana. Upon his return east, he left the survey to join an expedition to explore a northeastern region of Canada called Labrador.

Defining the Problem

In Labrador, Birdseye's interests quickly turned to commercial opportunities. Birdseye left the expedition when he saw the enormous profits the fur industry offered. He began to collect fox furs to sell. He traveled by dogsled over vast expanses of this Arctic region and became familiar with some of the local populations.

Birdseye observed the methods the indigenous people used to preserve fish and other animals. The extremely low temperatures allowed fish to freeze very quickly once they were removed from the water and thrown onto the ice. He discovered that when he thawed and cooked the frozen fish, they retained the same taste and texture as fresh fish.

This surprised Birdseye because the previous efforts in the United States to freeze food for storage had resulted in less than satisfactory products. No technology existed for freezing foods quickly; the slow freezing process allowed large ice crystals to form in and on the food while it froze. Birdseye understood that such crystal formation broke down the food's cellular structure and compromised its quality. The basic flash-freeze method, Birdseye concluded, prevented large ice crystals from forming, thereby retaining the food's original qualities—and its nutritional value.

Although based in Labrador, Birdseye continued to make trips to the United States. On one of these visits in 1915, he married Eleanor Gannett. The following year he moved his young family (including an infant son) to Labrador. He continued to hunt for furs and to travel great distances while his family lived in a three-room cabin in a remote wilderness.

Designing the Solution

Eager to provide the family with a well-rounded diet of good-tasting foods, Birdseye experimented with freezing various foods, including vegetables such as cabbage. He had brought a large quantity of fresh vegetables with him to Labrador. Once there, he applied a method similar to the one he had observed in preserving fish. He dipped the vegetables in brine (salt water) and then left them to flash-freeze in the frigid temperatures and high winds. The result was satisfactory, and the family had enough food to last through that winter.

After returning to the United States in 1917, Birdseye settled with his family first in Washington, DC, where he worked for a time as assistant to the president in the US Fisheries Association. In 1922, he moved the family to New York and pursued the wholesale fish business, starting Birdseye Seafoods, Inc. He set up his headquarters near the Fulton Street Market, where the city's fresh fish were brought every day. Birdseye was eager to develop a means of quick-freezing foods similar to the one he had observed in Labrador, without the benefit of the Arctic climate. In Birdseye's words, his aim was to combine "Eskimo knowledge and the scientists' theories and adapt them to quantity production."

With his wholesale business under way, Birdseye began experimenting in his home kitchen. Using an electric fan, buckets of brine, and cakes of ice, Birdseye tried various combinations until he arrived at a means of packing fresh food into cardboard

How Frozen Foods Began

Even though Clarence Birdseye proclaimed that frozen foods began in his kitchen in 1923, he was not the first person to freeze foods to preserve them. In 1626, the great English writer Francis Bacon experimented with preserving a chicken by stuffing it with snow. The bird remained preserved for some time, but Bacon developed pneumonia and died a month later—a discouraging beginning for frozen foods.

Advances in the freezing process came slowly. Around 1908, growers in California began to freeze fruits in a process called cold packing. They would add sugar to fruits or berries and then pack them in barrels in a kind of brine, or mixture, of ice and salt. This brine would preserve the food for transport to other parts of the country, where it might be stored for short periods before spoiling.

Not until the 1920s, however, with Clarence Birdseye's experiments in the freezing process, did the possibility of long-lasting boxes and flash-freezing them under high pressure. Birdseye later recalled, "Production of perishable foods, dressed at the point of production and quick-frozen in consumer packages, was initiated, so far as I am aware, in the kitchen of my own home late in 1923 when I experimentally packaged rabbit meat and fish fillets in candy boxes and froze the packages with dry ice."

Birdseye's two major innovations were to flash-freeze food in a manner that retained its original taste, texture, and appearance, and to do so in the same package in which that food was to be sold. He sought to perfect this process through further home experiments.

Applying the Solution

Birdseye Seafoods, Inc. did not last beyond its first year, but Birdseye persevered. The following year, living in Yorktown, New York, Birdseye came closer to perfecting the technique of using waxed cardboard to contain food that was then flash-frozen under high pressure. In 1924, he established a new firm, the General Seafoods Company.

preservation arrive. Birdseye made several important discoveries. First, he observed that flash-freezing food, or freezing food quickly, preserved the food's freshness and taste much better than allowing the food to freeze slowly. He devised a way to accomplish the flash-freezing of food in special waxed cardboard boxes that would be sold directly to consumers. Birdseye also introduced the first commercial process for blanching vegetables (immersing them briefly in boiling water) before freezing them. Blanching vegetables kills certain enzymes that can cause discoloration or create disagreeable flavors. When vegetables thus processed are thawed and reheated, they retain much of their original appearance, texture, flavor, and nutritional value. Thus, while Clarence Birdseye did not invent the process of freezing food, he did invent a method that allowed frozen food to expand into a vast industry.

In 1925, he moved his operation to larger facilities in Gloucester, Massachusetts. This Atlantic coast fishing town offered a prime opportunity to combine Birdseye's methods with a ready, abundant source of fresh fish. He continued experimenting with various freezing devices, eventually developing the first practical commercial freezer. Along with some other investors, Birdseye established the General Foods Company to function as the parent company for General Seafoods.

Having refined the method of freezing food, Birdseye set his sights on the equipment needed to apply this method on a mass scale. He developed a double-belt machine for quick freezing in 1926. At a weight of 20 tons (18 metric tons), however, this machine proved impractical to produce and transport. He worked to create a smaller machine, eventually coming up with a multiple-plate freezer that could be more easily moved. Foods packed in waxed cardboard boxes were frozen between two refrigerated plates under pressure.

To launch a frozen food industry along the lines he envisioned, Birdseye needed more funds to develop the necessary equipment. In 1929, he sold his company and all associated patents and trademarks for $22 million to Frosted Foods Company. The new company remained in Gloucester and took the name General Foods Corporation. Birdseye stayed on, and under his supervision researchers developed new technologies that further advanced the possibility of mass-produced frozen food. Among these was the use of coated cellophane to cover the containers in which the food had been frozen. The product name was changed to "Birds Eye," and Clarence Birdseye was put in charge of developing a new line to be called Birds Eye Frosted Foods. Birdseye's group managed to freeze more than one hundred different foods successfully. General Foods Corporation went on to dominate the frozen food market for years to come.

Soon General Foods Corporation was ready to begin test-marketing the new frozen products. The first test was done in Springfield, Massachusetts, on March 6, 1930. In eighteen separate stores, nearly thirty different types of frozen food—fish and meats, vegetables, and fruits—were made available to enthusiastic consumers.

During the Great Depression, many people had to wait in long lines like this one to get food. Birdseye's frozen foods helped feed hungry people.

Other tests in Syracuse and Rochester, New York, followed, and the public interest in frozen foods grew.

These test runs occurred during the Great Depression (ca. 1929–1940), a time when much of the United States was struggling financially and could not afford enough to eat. Although many people jumped at the chance to purchase relatively inexpensive food that they otherwise would have been unable to obtain because it was out of season, most retailers could not afford the available freezers that would allow them to keep supplies on hand. Recognizing this obstacle, Clarence Birdseye developed an inexpensive freezer display case that he offered to lease to retailers for just a few dollars a month. This was the first step in launching a regional frozen food industry. By the late 1930s, some sixty Birds Eye Frosted Foods—vegetables, fruits, and meats—were available in refrigerated displays throughout the Northeast. Americans were spending approximately $150 million a year on frozen foods by 1940.

Birdseye was eager to expand his distribution beyond the northeastern United States. In 1944, he leased insulated railroad cars that could transport his products nationwide, and the frozen food industry was now in full swing. By the end of the decade, the offerings had expanded to include hors d'oeuvres, complete frozen meals, and, of course, frozen pizza. As frozen foods caught on, refrigerator technology adapted, giving more and more space to freezers. Soon Americans were buying separate freezers.

The Impact of the Solution on Society

Although most of Birdseye's inventions were related to his work perfecting the process of freezing foods, he made contributions in other food-related products as well. One of these involved a method for dehydrating food that resulted in small food packets that could be easily carried or stored. This technology has been important to consumers around the world and has proved essential for hikers and astronauts.

Birdseye worked in other areas and received many patents. One was for a kind of heat lamp with superior filaments for keeping food warm. His attention focused on other electrical items; in 1935, he formed the Birdseye Electric Company, which he sold to the Sylvania Company in 1939. He also received a patent for a kind of whale harpoon and another for an electrical fishing reel for commercial fishermen that allowed them to fish at greater depths.

Toward the end of his career, Birdseye's interests again shifted. Working on a plantation in Peru, he sought to improve methods for manufacturing paper. He developed a method to convert sugarcane into paper pulp much more quickly.

Birdseye died of a heart attack in 1956, at the age of sixty-nine. In all he had received about three hundred patents in the United States and abroad, but by the time of his death he was universally known as the father of frozen food. Birdseye was able to witness the thriving frozen food industry of which he had dreamed in Labrador more than forty years earlier.

The legacy of Birds Eye foods continues today. Around the world, products continue to be sold with the Birds Eye name, in honor of the man who invented them and revolutionized the way people froze food. Birdseye made significant improvements to food preservation practices and paved the way for other pioneers to perfect the art.

Timeline

1886
Clarence Birdseye born in Brooklyn, New York

1912
Birdseye joins an expedition to Labrador, Canada, where he develops an interest in flash-freezing food

1923
Birdseye develops the process of commercial flash-freezing in his home

1924
Birdseye establishes the General Seafoods Company

1926
Birdseye develops the double-belt machine for quick-freezing food

1929
Birdseye sells his company, patents, and trademarks to Frosted Foods Company

1930
Frozen food products are test-marketed for the first time in Springfield, Massachusetts

1944
Birdseye begins distributing his frozen products across the United States

1956
Birdseye dies

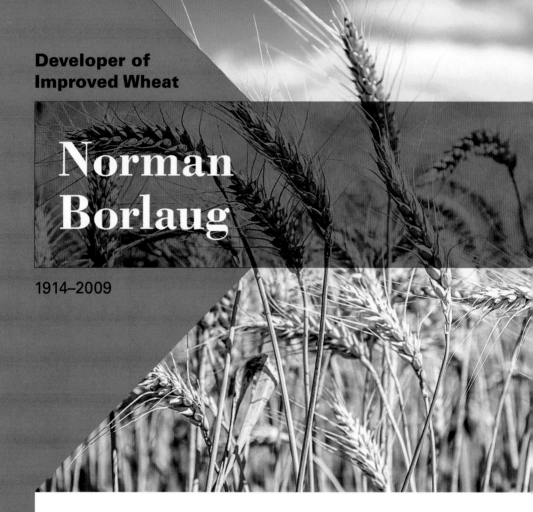

Norman Borlaug

1914–2009

Every year thousands of people in developing countries struggle
to live. There have been many efforts to help these people sustain
themselves by using agricultural techniques such as farming.
Likewise, many scientists have tried to invent new products that
will make growing certain crops easier. Norman Borlaug was a
person who developed new varieties of grain that could be grown
in struggling nations. For his work, he is well known and revered.

An Inventor Begins

Norman Ernest Borlaug was born on a farm near Cresco, Iowa,
on March 25, 1914. His parents, Henry and Clara, were both

Norwegian immigrants, part of a close community of Norwegian farmers. Having experienced hunger in Norway, they had immigrated to the United States eager to make a better life. Their concerns about hunger—even starvation—left a strong impression on young Borlaug.

Borlaug attended a one-room rural school near Cresco through the eighth grade. He then attended Cresco High School, where he began to develop a strong interest in crop and soil science. He also excelled in athletics in high school. Borlaug graduated from Cresco High School in 1932. He then entered the University of Minnesota in Minneapolis, earning a bachelor of science degree in forestry in 1937. While working part-time as a forester, Borlaug stayed on at the university, earning a master of science degree in 1939 and a doctorate in 1942, both in plant **pathology**. He was strongly influenced by Elvin Charles Stakman, a professor of plant pathology. Borlaug had encountered Stakman while an undergraduate and came to regard him as his mentor. Under Stakman's direction, Borlaug completed a dissertation on a type of fungal rot to which flax was susceptible.

Upon receiving his PhD, Borlaug moved to Wilmington, Delaware, to take a job with E.I. DuPont de Nemours and Company. His job at DuPont was to examine the effects of various new chemicals that had been introduced into agricultural practice. He also worked with a team commissioned by the US government to develop superior products for preserving and transporting foods to troops during World War II. Borlaug remained at DuPont until 1944.

Defining the Problem

In 1944, Borlaug joined a team headed by George Harrar and funded by the Rockefeller Foundation to assist in a crisis in Mexican crop production. After a series of wheat crop failures in Mexico, the Mexican ministry of agriculture asked the US government for assistance. Borlaug was appointed director of the Cooperative Wheat Research and Production Program in Mexico. His mission was to develop new methods of soil use and to create more suitable strains of wheat for cultivation in Mexico.

Designing the Solution

Wheat varieties and methods of cultivation had remained virtually unchanged in Mexico since the sixteenth century, when the Spanish conquistadors had introduced the grain to the region. After years of adapting to poor soil and cultivation, which required grain crops to compete with tall weeds for sunlight, the wheat had become too tall and thin-stemmed. As a result, wheat routinely fell over before it could be harvested—a trait known as lodging. Borlaug's team sought to breed a species of high-yield, disease-resistant wheat that was more suitable to the Mexican climate. At the same time, he worked with Mexican agricultural scientists to improve soil management and growing methods.

Results soon showed that Borlaug's ideas held great promise, not just for Mexico but for all regions with poor cultivation practices and difficult growing conditions. By 1948, Mexican farmers were growing enough wheat to sustain the country's population without imports. Increased irrigation and fertilizer use, combined with improved wheat and soil maintenance, produced a superior crop.

At the same time, however, these fertilizers (especially the nitrogen that caused rapid growth spurts) began to yield wheat with seed heads larger than the thin stalks could support. As a result, wheat stalks again began to lodge once they reached a certain height, causing significant loss.

Borlaug was again called upon to develop a strain that could support the larger wheat heads. He created a hybrid, using the Mexican variety crossed with a Japanese dwarf variety, resulting in shorter plants. By 1963, nearly all of Mexico's wheat was the semi-dwarf variety Borlaug had developed. With harvests as much as six times greater than those of twenty years earlier, Mexico had become a net exporter of wheat.

Applying the Solution

Soon thereafter, Borlaug's newly created research team, the International Center for Maize and Wheat Improvement, applied its discoveries to other parts of the world. As conflict continued between

Norman Borlaug, in 1970, holding up stalks of crossbred wheat

Norman Borlaug

India and Pakistan over the semiautonomous region of Kashmir in the mid-1960s, Borlaug was called upon to help stem the widening famine caused by agricultural shortages in both countries. Beginning in 1962, Borlaug's team had begun to send seeds of his improved semi-dwarf varieties for test growth in India. The following year Borlaug visited India to inspect the results of several new varieties at multiple locations across the Indian subcontinent. In 1965, Borlaug's team sent about 450 tons (408 metric tons) of seeds to be distributed in Pakistan and India.

Although the team's efforts encountered a variety of logistical and bureaucratic obstacles in the United States, India, and Pakistan, the seeds were finally planted. The yield of the first crop, although less than Borlaug expected owing to damage to the seeds in shipment, was higher than any the subcontinent had ever achieved. Both countries dramatically increased their import of Borlaug's seeds in 1966, and

A New Kind of Revolution

After his success developing new strains of wheat suitable for growing in Mexico, Borlaug expanded his efforts to help other countries struggling to feed their populations. His work in India and Pakistan in the 1960s led to what has been described as a "green revolution," referring to the introduction of farming methods that allow areas of the world with few successful crops to become self-sufficient in crop production.

Borlaug championed the use of chemical fertilizers and pesticides to improve crop yields. However, many people regard this kind of agriculture as anything but "green." Crop varieties that rely on fertilizers and pesticides force farmers in developing countries to purchase those resources; the cost, such critics maintain, extends well beyond farmers. Chemical fertilizers and pesticides, they say, adversely affect the entire environment, and they argue that introducing a single crop variety into a region threatens that region's biodiversity. If a single crop variety over a large area were to be attacked by a new fungus or insect, all of that region's food production could be destroyed, whereas by 1968 they were able to produce enough wheat to provide their own seed stock for the following year's planting. Wheat yields in both India and Pakistan approximately doubled between 1965, the year Borlaug first planted there, and 1970.

Despite grave warnings in the mid-1960s about widespread starvation in the world, food production has outpaced the sharp growth in population. Borlaug's innovations were said to have caused a "green revolution," and many people credit him with saving more than a billion lives. For his work in improving agricultural methods and introducing improved wheat varieties to populations threatened with starvation, Norman Borlaug was awarded the Nobel Peace Prize in 1970.

Criticism and Theories

Borlaug's views about agricultural advances have not gone unchallenged. Many critics—both agriculturalists and ecologists—maintain that his biotechnological methods and use of large-scale

in regions where biodiversity is made a priority, some crops might be susceptible to new attacks while some would remain immune.

Borlaug argued that traditional agricultural methods, especially in regions where growing conditions are difficult, simply cannot meet the needs of the people living in those regions. Biotechnology allows farmers to produce higher yields using less land. In an interview with the American Institute of Biological Sciences, Boralug responded to criticism of his approach in Africa and South Asia. He noted, "If we had continued practicing conventional farming, we would have cut down millions of acres of forest, thereby destroying wildlife habitat, in order to increase cropland to produce enough food for an escalating population. And we would have to use more herbicides in more fields, which would damage the environment even more. Technology allows us to have less impact on soil erosion, biodiversity, wildlife, forests, and grasslands."

Norman Borlaug poses with his wife, Margaret, after receiving the Nobel
Peace Prize in 1970.

monocultural (single-crop) farming techniques harm the environment and threaten biodiversity. His programs depend on a high level of inorganic fertilizers and pesticides, leading many to question the long-term sustainability of his methods. In response, Borlaug argued that his efforts have been carried out on behalf of people in emergencies and that his approach to addressing those emergencies agriculturally has been consistent with responsible environmental principles.

His position was perhaps best summed up in what has become known as the Borlaug hypothesis. According to this theory, if crop yields are increased in already established agricultural regions, the need to create new farmland by deforestation and other assaults on our ecosystems can be reduced or even eliminated. The use of "inputs" (fertilizer, pesticides, and irrigation) is defensible because without them crop production cannot be maximized on existing farmland. Borlaug argued that organic farming methods, which minimize or completely reject such inputs, are inadequate to the demands of a rapidly increasing world population.

The Impact of the Solution on Society

Although he retired from most of his major posts in the early 1980s, Norman Borlaug remained active in various US and international projects into the twenty-first century. Beginning in 1984, he became professor of international agriculture at Texas A&M University. That same year, he helped found the Sasakawa Africa Association (SAA; named after Japanese businessman Ryoichi Sasakawa) to extend the methods Borlaug had developed for use in South Asia to address famine in Africa. The program's efforts resulted in increased crop yields in several African countries.

In 1986, Borlaug established the World Food Prize to recognize important contributions to food production methods around the world. Borlaug himself received, in addition to the Nobel Peace Prize, the US Presidential Medal of Freedom (1977) and numerous other awards. In 2005, at a special White House ceremony, he received one of three National Medals of Science for Biological Sciences— the nation's highest honor for scientists. Sadly, in 2009 he passed away at the age of ninety-five.

For his contributions to fighting world hunger and his achievements with his product around the globe, Borlaug will always be remembered and celebrated. He was a pioneer in modern agricultural technology, and his efforts continue through the legacy he left behind.

Timeline

1914
Norman Borlaug born in Iowa

1942
Borlaug earns a doctorate in plant pathology from the University of Minnesota

1944
Borlaug is appointed as director of the Cooperative Wheat Research and Production Program

1948
Using Borlaug's improved strain of wheat, Mexican farmers are able to grow sufficient wheat to feed their country

1962
Borlaug and his team begin testing his improved wheat in India

1970
Borlaug is awarded the Nobel Peace Prize

1984
Borlaug becomes a professor of international agriculture at Texas A&M University

2005
Borlaug is awarded the National Medal of Science for Biological Sciences

2009
Borlaug dies

Jacques Brandenberger

1872–1954

Sometimes inventions are created by accident. An inventor might intend to solve a problem, and through experimentation, an entirely new product forms. Such was the case with the invention of cellophane. This clear plastic wrap resulted from an attempt to create a product to clean tablecloths. Little did the inventor, Jacques Brandenberger, know that his "mistake" would lead to such a popular and essential product for food sanitation.

Starting Out

Jacques Brandenberger was born in Zurich, Switzerland, in 1872. He became interested in chemistry early and proved to be an exceptional student, earning his doctorate from the University of Bern at age twenty-two.

Brandenberger soon moved to France, where he spent the next several years working as a dye expert for textile companies in Normandy and then Remiremont. During this time, he developed a new process to **mercerize** cotton, which involves treating the cotton with chemicals to shrink it to improve its strength and luster.

Brandenberger's hometown of Zurich, Switzerland, in the late 1890s

Defining the Problem

One day in 1900, Brandenberger was sitting in a restaurant when another patron spilled wine onto the tablecloth. Since at the time tablecloths were made of untreated fabric, the waiter had to change the cloth.

The resulting film was then passed through a number of baths—all part of the same machine—designed to wash, bleach, and soften it. Finally, the film was dried and rolled into spools. As cellophane manufacturing became more sophisticated and specialized, additional steps were added to coat the film to make it moisture-proof or able to be heat-sealed.

Applying the Solution

In 1912, Brandenberger had discovered a commercial market: the eyepieces of gas masks. Not only was the film lighter than glass; it did not shatter, and so it was safer. In addition, because the film absorbed water vapor, eyepieces made of it did not fog up as did glass eyepieces.

Brandenberger founded a company, La Cellophane, and gave the same name to his invention. The name was a combination of the words "cellulose" and "diaphane," a French word meaning "transparent." In 1917, Brandenberger transferred his patents to La Cellophane Société Anonyme, his cellophane-manufacturing enterprise located near Paris.

In 1923, Brandenberger sold the rights to produce and distribute cellophane in the Americas to the chemical company DuPont. Four years later, DuPont's scientist William Hale Charch developed a way

Monumental Achievement in Waterproofing

Although by the time Charch added water resistance to cellophane the product was already being used as a wrapping, the development of moisture-proof cellophane made it the wrapping of choice for many products—especially food. Before the invention of moisture-proof cellophane, food was usually wrapped in paper, which was neither waterproof nor airtight. As a result, if the air was dry, food dried out quickly; if the air was humid, food would get damp. Most food could not be stored for long and remain palatable, even if kept cold. Charch's added touch of water-resistance proved a valuable trait for the product to have and propelled it into the limelight of everyday living.

to make cellophane moisture-proof. Charch coated both sides of a cellophane sheet with extremely thin layers of resin, plastic, and wax. The process made cellophane almost completely resistant to water in both liquid and vapor form.

The new cellophane kept the food's moisture in and other moisture out. Food manufacturers, restaurateurs, and ordinary people quickly discovered that food wrapped in cellophane stayed fresh much longer. In addition, cellophane wrapping improved food safety because it helped keep the juices of raw meat, poultry, and fish from contaminating other foods. Within just a few years of its invention, moisture-proof cellophane could be found in most kitchens.

The new industry was an enormous windfall for DuPont. In 1928, the first year moisture-proof cellophane went on the market, the company sold about $3.7 million worth of cellophane. By 1950, DuPont was selling $99.3 million worth of cellophane every year, with $89.9 million fully attributable to sales of moisture-proof cellophane.

Brandenberger continued to lead La Cellophane Société until 1953, when he became ill with a kidney ailment. In October of that year, he moved back to Zurich to seek treatment, and he died there in July 1954.

The Impact of the Solution on Society

By the 1960s, advances in plastics allowed for the creation of transparent films that were cheaper to make than cellulose-based cellophane and eventually replaced it. Nonetheless, Brandenberger's term "cellophane" lives on to mean any transparent, waterproof film.

Cellophane has done more than improve food safety and keep leftovers fresh. Since food wrapped in cellophane stays edible longer, perishables no longer need to be grown or harvested locally, and that fact, combined with the modern transportation network, has helped radically change the food industry.

Baked goods, meats, frozen meals, and other foods can now be produced in a central facility, wrapped in cellophane, and shipped to grocery stores or restaurants across the nation. As a result, food production is no longer the business of many scattered local providers. Instead, it is an industry dominated by large-scale corporate producers.

Brandenberger may have developed cellophane by accident, but there is no denying that his accident became an important part of modern-day living. Without cellophane, the world of produce and how it is stored would be very different than the one in which we are living today.

Timeline

1872
Jacques Brandenberger born in Zurich, Switzerland

1894
Brandenberger earns a doctorate from the University of Bern

1900
Brandenberger begins experimenting with cellulose to create a stain-proof tablecloth

1908
Brandenberger perfects a manufacturing process for his cellulose film

1912
Brandenberger begins to make eyepieces for gas masks out of his film

1923
Brandenberger sells the rights to produce and distribute cellophane in the Americas to DuPont Company

1927
William Hale Charch, a scientist at DuPont, discovers a way to make cellophane moisture-proof

1954
Brandenberger dies

Edwin Beard Budding

1795–1846

When one thinks of lawn care, one of the first machines to spring to mind is most likely a lawn mower. Lawn mowers are used to cut grass, making lawns appear smooth and well manicured. Today, many people in the United States and elsewhere take care of their lawns by using these machines that cut the lawn for them. Sometimes you sit on these machines, whereas other machines require you to push them. Prior to the nineteenth century, however, lawn mowers did not exist. It was inventor Edwin Beard Budding who created the device and revolutionized the way people looked after their property. Without this invention, lawn care would be very different from what it is now.

Little Known Beginnings

Very little is known about Edwin Beard Budding. He was born in 1795, in Stroud, a small village near Gloucestershire, England. In the nineteenth century, Stroud was the center of England's growing textile industry.

Budding was working as an engineer when he first developed the lawn mower. He was thirty-five years old when he received his patent.

Defining the Problem

Lawns as we know them in contemporary times did not exist until the 1700s. Earlier, most homes were bordered by gardens or natural grasses and weeds, the length of which was typically determined not by a mechanical device but by grazing animals, like sheep and cattle. The first formal lawns were created in France. These lawns, which were sometimes called pleasure grounds, were kept by the French aristocracy, primarily as pleasant surroundings for outdoor games.

The lawn mowers of that era were little more than repurposed farm or gardening equipment, such as **scythes**, which were used to reap wheat and other crops, and shears, scissor-like tools that were typically used for gardening. Maintaining a lawn with such basic tools was tedious—it took considerable effort to cut an entire lawn by hand. For example, in the eighteenth century, fifty men wielding scythes were needed to cut the lawns of Blenheim Palace, near Oxford, England, and the lawns had to be cut every ten days. The process was also erratic. For a clean cut, the scythe or shears had to strike the grass at a consistent angle and speed. Often, the results were uneven, with scraggly areas of uncut grass and bald areas where a gardener cut too close.

Despite the arduous work necessary to maintain a lawn, the idea soon spread to England and other parts of Europe. From the start, the lawn was a sign of wealth, nobility, and social status— and, as some historians suggest, a symbol of humanity's power over nature. However, as the popularity of lawns spread, it became clear that a different mechanism would have to be created to cut lawns smoothly and in less time.

The streets of Stroud, Gloucestershire, England, where Budding was born, ca. 1910

Designing the Solution

More than a century had passed since the advent of the first lawns before Budding devised a new and improved way to cut them. Budding took inspiration from the **nap**-cutting machines used by textile manufacturers to trim stray threads from carpets, leaving a smooth, uniform finish. His mower had a series of blades arranged around a cylinder and cut grass much the same way that scissors cut fabric. The blades were positioned perpendicular to the ground. Today, this design is known as a reel mower.

Soon after being granted a patent, Budding went into business with a man named John Ferrabee. Their mowers, made of cast iron, had a 19-inch (48.2 cm) cylinder; they were so heavy that they had to be pushed or pulled by horses. Within two years, other companies were producing mowers under licensing agreements. The most successful of these companies was Ransomes, which is still in existence today.

Within a decade of Budding's patent, more than a thousand of his mowers had been sold. By the 1850s, however, Budding's patent had lapsed, and a variety of lawn mowers began to arrive on the market.

The first reel lawn mower would not earn a US patent until 1868, nearly forty years after Budding's invention. US Patent No. 73,807 was awarded to a Connecticut man named Amariah Hills. Hills sold his rights to the patent in the 1870s.

Not long after Hills was granted a patent, Elwood McGuire of Richmond, Indiana, developed a hand-operated mower. Though not the first hand-operated mower, it was one of the first lightweight models. It was also easier to use and was less expensive than previous mowers.

The late nineteenth century saw a wave of developments in mowers. In 1885, more than fifty thousand lawn mowers were being produced in the United States each year. By 1888, the US Patent Office had granted 138 lawn mower patents.

Then, on May 9, 1899, an African-American inventor named John Albert Burr was granted US Patent No. 624,749 on yet another improvement in lawn mowers. Unlike the reel mowers, Burr's mower had a rotary blade, which spun parallel to the ground. His design also included traction wheels, making it possible to mow closer to the edges of buildings and walls.

When mechanical power came to lawn mowers, shortly after the turn of the twentieth century, rotary blade mowers adapted. Another advance in rotary mowers came in 1940, with Leonard Goodall's invention, the power push-pull mower. Indeed, the advent of power rotary mowers left behind the reel mower, a cumbersome relic of the past.

Applying the Solution

Although mower innovation continued through the 1940s, not until the 1950s, with America's postwar economic boom, the expansion of the suburbs, and the advent of lightweight plastics, did lawn mowers

Today, lawn mowers can be pushed or controlled by sitting on them.

become extremely popular. Mowers were more usable and more affordable, so the middle class could have the lawns once reserved for the rich. In 1951, more than 1.1 million power mowers were manufactured in the United States.

The Impact of the Solution on Society

Today, some lawn enthusiasts are returning to hand-powered mowers. Old-fashioned mowers are particularly attractive to people who are concerned about the noise and air pollution created by electric- or gas-powered models. (The Environmental Protection Agency has estimated that power mowers contribute roughly 5 percent of the nation's air pollution each year.) Like many nineteenth-century inventions, versions of mowers made by Budding, Burr, Hills, or McGuire are prized by collectors and are sold for hundreds of dollars at antiques shows.

Inventors of Food and Agriculture Technology

Budding's invention started a trend of other similar devices. Eventually, his concept morphed into many different kinds of lawn-mowing machines. It is because of him and other pioneering inventors in the field that lawn mowing has become so popular and is now almost an essential part of American life.

Timeline

1795
Edwin Beard Budding born in Stroud, England

1830
Budding receives his patent for a lawn mower; soon after this, he goes into business with John Ferrabee

1846
Budding dies

1850s
Budding's patent lapses, making way for a variety of other lawn mowers

1868
Amariah Hills is awarded a US patent for his reel lawn mower

1899
John Albert Burr patents his rotary blade lawn mower, which will serve as a model for modern machines

**Inventor of
New Plant Varieties**

Luther
Burbank

1849–1926

Around the world, there are people who spend their entire lives dedicating themselves to one area of study. Inventions that come from these people sometimes have a profound impact on certain industries. The industry of food and agriculture is no different. One **horticulturalist** named Luther Burbank is responsible for bringing new types of plants and foods into society. Most notably, he is responsible for breeding the Russet Burbank potato, now called the Idaho potato. Today, it is one of the most popular potatoes used in the United States.

An Inventor Begins

Born on March 7, 1849, the thirteenth of fifteen children, Burbank grew up on his family's farm in Lancaster, Massachusetts. He showed an avid interest in plant life at an early age. Burbank's formal schooling ended after high school at Lancaster Academy, but his passion for the natural world led him to study closely all life-forms in his environment, noting the smallest differences between many varieties of plants.

Defining the Problem

Burbank also spent long hours in the Lancaster public library, where he devoured every book on natural history he could find. The book that most interested him, and in fact would change his life forever, was Charles Darwin's *On the Variation of Animals and Plants Under Domestication* (1868). Burbank learned in this book how breeders could select desirable traits or characteristics in domestic plants and animals, resulting in improved types of vegetables, for example. "It was without question the most inspiring book I had ever read," Burbank later recalled. It certainly was powerfully influential for his entire career.

Shortly after his father's death in 1868, Burbank used his small inheritance to purchase 17 acres (7 hectares) of land near Lunenburg, Massachusetts. He decided to grow vegetables to sell at local farmers' markets and enjoyed success in this endeavor. People in the area soon recognized the superiority of his produce. Burbank also set to work applying Darwin's ideas to the plants available to him.

Designing the Solution

One of Burbank's first experiments led him to develop in 1872 a type of potato he considered to be superior to any that he had seen or eaten. Although Burbank did not always keep detailed records of his discoveries, he did leave in his journal the story of how he created the Russet Burbank.

Potatoes commonly do not produce seeds. Rather, farmers and gardeners grow potatoes by planting a portion of another potato, or **tuber**, in the ground. On his land in Massachusetts in 1872, Burbank

Luther Burbank in his garden of Shasta daisies

was growing the Early Rose variety of potato. He discovered a rare seed ball growing on one of his vines, and he decided to harvest the seeds for planting the following spring.

After planting the twenty-three seeds, Burbank saw that the plants and tubers that grew from them differed in size and quantity. While all twenty-three seeds did sprout, a few seedlings appeared superior to the Early Rose parent. He eventually identified one plant that produced the largest and most abundant potatoes, and by the summer of 1874, he realized he had come up with a potato that could produce three times as many tubers as existing varieties. He decided to introduce this potato to the public.

After being turned down by one nurseryman, Burbank approached seed dealer J.H. Gregory in Marblehead, Massachusetts, sending him a sample of his new "creation." Burbank said he would sell the stock of these potatoes for $500 (around $10,600 US in 2014). Gregory agreed to pay $150 (around $3,100 US in 2014). With the money, Burbank bought a train ticket to California, where he lived the rest of his life. With Gregory's permission, he took with him ten of the tubers from this superior potato. Those ten potatoes Burbank transported to California in 1875 became the basis for the Burbank variety in western states.

Gregory named the new potato variety after Burbank and began selling it to the public. Burbank wrote that these mutated potatoes exhibited a "modified coat [that is] particularly resistant to blight, which gives it exceptional value." Within just a few years, the Burbank became extremely popular in the West, and by the time he died, Burbank's potato, known as the Idaho, was the preferred potato around the world.

Applying the Solution

Burbank moved to Santa Rosa and continued his work in plant breeding. He purchased a small plot of land there and set up greenhouses, later buying several more acres to carry out his work on a larger scale. His experiments in grafting, **hybridization**, and crossbreeding led to many new varieties of fruits, vegetables, and ornamental flowers.

Burbank had no scientific training, yet he had read enough of the scientific literature about hybridization to put him on solid ground. He did not consider himself a scientist, and his methods would seem unusual to many horticultural scientists. Moreover, his interests did not lie in the advancement of scientific knowledge about hybridization in and of itself, but rather in producing more and better varieties of plants than were currently available. His allegiance was to people and local markets. As a result, Burbank left relatively few detailed records about the processes he used to develop his many plant crosses (or hybrids). He would often discard whatever notes he had kept during his experiments once he achieved his desired result.

Burbank imported as many plants as he could from other parts of the world, and he set about making as many crosses of these plants as possible. Often, he would crossbreed plants for the sole purpose of trying to make the largest possible variation, or "perturbation," as he called it, from the original plants. He was fascinated with the entire range of possibilities in crossbreeding, and he was always looking for favorable, unexpected results to emerge from unusual combinations. Sometimes this approach was unsuccessful, as when he attempted to cross an almond with a peach. Other such efforts led to more useful

An Eye for Plums

As a child, Luther Burbank developed an understanding of plants based on his close observation of minute differences between plant types. In later life he learned to tell by looking at a plum seedling's leaves whether that strain was likely to produce the best-tasting fruit. How was he able to know for sure that these very young plants would in fact produce superior fruit when they were fully grown?

Once Burbank had identified a few plum seedlings that he thought would produce more or better-tasting plums, he would graft those

Burbank created heartier plums by a process called grafting.

Inventors of Food and Agriculture Technology

and profitable plants, such as his creation of several varieties of spineless cacti for feeding livestock in arid regions.

Burbank was a highly imaginative plant breeder. As his skills developed, he was guided more by his perceptions than by any prescribed methods of hybridization. His powers of perception allowed him to recognize desirable plant characteristics that other breeders had overlooked and to make connections between different characteristics that others did not take into account. He often recognized desirable variations in their very earliest stages of formation, whereas most other scientists were forced to wait for plants to be full grown before assessing their desirability.

seedlings onto the stock, or branches, of a mature plum tree. Grafting involves attaching the seedling to another tree by slicing an opening into both parts and joining the two using a special kind of fluid or tape. As many as fifty or sixty scions, or grafted young plants, were attached to a single adult plum stock. A single plum tree, then, might have dozens of different plum types growing on it at the same time.

Instead of waiting seven years to see the quality of fruit, Burbank could see the results of his seedlings in only one or two years. He could then determine which branches produced larger or sweeter fruit, which ones bore fruit the soonest, and which ones made their fruit later in the season. All of these characteristics might be desirable under different circumstances, and Burbank could select a particular variety for a particular market or need. Burbank tested more than thirty thousand plum seedling types and grafted the most promising ones onto adult trees—in one case, he had six hundred plum grafts on a single parent stock. In this way he produced 113 new varieties of plum trees.

Although Luther Burbank did not invent this method of grafting, his acute powers of observation and ability to make important connections between plant characteristics led him to use grafting to a greater degree and in a more refined manner than had been previously done.

For example, in examining many different strains of plum seedlings, or young plants, Burbank learned to recognize the connections between leaf characteristics of a seedling and the type of fruit the mature tree would eventually produce. He took note of almost imperceptible differences between seedling leaf types and selected those that indicated to him that the full-grown tree would produce the plumpest, sweetest plums. The other seedlings he destroyed.

Famous for His Work

As his reputation as a master plant breeder grew, Burbank's fame spread across the country and beyond. Unlike many inventors who toil in obscurity, Burbank was quite famous in his lifetime and became friendly with Thomas Edison, Henry Ford, Helen Keller, and Jack London, to name a few. He attained a kind of celebrity as a freethinker—an independent spirit who celebrated humans' connections to nature rather than participating in organized religious observance. His operation at Santa Rosa became a pilgrimage destination for people all over the world. Although he married twice, Burbank had no children.

Burbank wrote several books about his work. Especially notable is the twelve-volume *Luther Burbank: His Methods and Discoveries and Their Practical Applications* (1914–1915) and an eight-volume set, *How Plants Are Trained to Work for Man* (1921). In 1893, Burbank began publishing a series of catalogs, *New Creations*, intended to introduce the general public to his new plant varieties. The first, and most famous, *New Creations in Fruits and Flowers*, brought him international acclaim. Some critics, however, observed that Burbank appeared to claim powers for himself as a plant creator that should be reserved for God. Burbank responded to such complaints by saying that his "creations" were made within the framework allowed by God's creation, nature.

Burbank died of a heart attack on April 11, 1926. He was buried beneath a cedar of Lebanon tree that he had planted as a seedling.

The Impact of the Solution on Society

Considering the vast industry based on the Idaho potato, it is amazing that Burbank's profit amounted to a train ticket to California. Nevertheless, his legacy is unquestioned. Despite many attempts by potato breeders in Idaho to develop an improvement, no variety has yet managed to equal the Russet Burbank potato.

The Russet Burbank potato continues to have great success in the marketplace. It is used to make every type of potato and was for many years the potato of choice for McDonald's restaurants. The Russet Burbank has changed the way people consume potatoes and has made a big difference in the way plants are cultivated and bred. Burbank's legacy continues in the plant he became most known for creating.

Timeline

1849
Luther Burbank born in Lancaster, Massachusetts

1868
Burbank purchases a small farm in Lunenburg, Massachusetts

1872
Burbank develops the Russet Burbank, or Idaho, potato

1875
Burbank moves to Santa Rosa, California, where he conducts further experiments in horticulture

1893
Burbank begins publishing a series of catalogs, called *New Creations*

1901
Burbank introduces his Shasta daisy

1914–1915
Burbank publishes a twelve-volume book series on his work

1926
Burbank dies

George Washington Carver

ca. 1865–1943

Some inventors earn great fame during their lives, although they might have begun in relative obscurity. Their accomplishments continue long after they have passed away. A great contributor to food and agricultural technology was George Washington Carver, a man born a slave but who became one of the United States' most accomplished and celebrated inventors. His name is remembered today, and his achievements are noted and respected.

Carver's Start

George Washington Carver was born on a farm near Diamond, Missouri, sometime between 1860 and 1865. His parents were slaves, and records of slave births were not kept reliably, so even

George Washington Carver poses in a laboratory ca. 1935.

Carver did not know his exact birth date. Soon after his birth, his father was killed in an accident while hauling wood on an ox wagon. As a baby, Carver, along with his mother and sister, was kidnapped by Confederate soldiers. Moses Carver, who owned the farm, reputedly got the baby back in exchange for a $300 racehorse, but the mother and sister were never found.

Young Carver barely survived the ordeal. Ill with whooping cough at the time, he then developed a respiratory condition that left him permanently frail and sickly. A doctor examined him and concluded that he would die before the age of twenty-one. As a result, Moses Carver and his wife did not expect young Carver to help with the heavier farm chores. Instead, he spent much of his time wandering the farm; Carver later recalled talking to flowers, playing with insects, and growing plants. His understanding of plants quickly earned him the nickname "plant doctor," and neighbors brought him their sick specimens to nurse back to health.

The area where the Carvers lived provided no schools for black people, so the Carvers taught George to read and write. When he was about ten or eleven, they allowed him to move 8 miles (12 km) away to the nearest town, Neosho, to attend school there. Carver discovered that he loved learning and said it "sharpened my appetite for more knowledge." Nevertheless, Carver took another twenty years to educate himself fully. During this time, he did whatever work he

Improving Soil

Nitrogen is one of the most common chemical elements and makes up around 78 percent of Earth's atmosphere. Although nitrogen is essential to life, plants and animals cannot use it straight from the air. Instead, they have to take in nitrogen-based compounds and break those down to get the nitrogen they need. Plants absorb these compounds from the soil to make proteins that help them grow. Animals eat the plants and use their nitrogen to make their own proteins. Bacteria help return nitrogen to the soil by breaking down dying plants and animals and animal waste. This enables the "nitrogen cycle" to repeat itself.

George Washington Carver made a great discovery when he realized that the nitrogen in the soil in southern states like Alabama had become depleted. Growing cotton every year in the same fields was a major cause. Carver's idea was to grow other crops in those could to support himself. He ran a laundry and worked as a cook, telegraph operator, and farmhand. He later wrote: "For quite one-month, I lived on prayer, beef suet and cornmeal, and quite often being without the suet and meal."

Finally, in his late twenties, Carver managed to finish his high school education in Minneapolis, Kansas. When a neighboring university refused to enroll him because he was black, he enrolled at Simpson College in Indianola, Iowa, in 1890. There he studied piano and art. One of his paintings from this time, of yucca and cactus plants, was exhibited at the Chicago world's fair in 1893. Carver transferred to Iowa State College of Agriculture and Mechanic Arts (now called Iowa State University) in 1891, earning his bachelor's degree in agricultural science in 1894 and his master's degree in 1896. He never grumbled about how long his education had taken: "There is no shortcut to achievement. Life requires thorough preparation—veneer isn't worth anything."

After graduation, Carver joined the college faculty and soon earned a reputation for his work in the field of botany. Before long, he came to the attention of Booker T. Washington, a pioneering educator

fields (crop rotation) so that nitrogen and other nutrients could be restored to the soil. This helped in two ways: it improved the soil and it produced important new crops that brought other economic benefits.

The legumes peanuts and soybeans and the tuber sweet potato are examples of plants that contain special "nitrogen-fixing" bacteria in the **nodules** of their roots. These bacteria absorb nitrogen from the air and convert it into nitrogen compounds that plants can use. When the legumes die or are harvested, their roots and the nitrogen they hold remain in the soil; when other crops (such as cotton) are planted in the fields where the nitrogen has been restored, they are able to utilize the newly refreshed soil. For the nitrogen cycle to be most efficient, growing different crops in different places each year is required. This process is called crop rotation.

in Alabama. Washington believed that education was the best way to help blacks gain a foothold in an economic system that had long been closed to them. Washington had helped found Tuskegee Institute (now Tuskegee University) in 1881 to put these ideas into practice. When he heard about Carver's work, he invited him to become director of Tuskegee's Department of Agricultural Research in 1896.

Defining the Problem

This job gave Carver an opportunity to explore ideas for managing the soil and growing crops in more productive ways. Agriculture in the South was in something of a crisis at the time. The enormous expansion in the number of acres planted in cotton during the nineteenth century had exhausted the soil in some areas, making growing crops more difficult. Also, a beetle called the boll weevil, which attacks **cotton bolls**, had thrived in conditions where only one crop was grown. Such difficulties had ruined some growers and caused economic problems for others, many of them black, whose livelihood depended on cotton.

Carver realized that if he could find smarter ways of using the soil and teach these methods to farmers, he could improve agriculture and people's lives at the same time. As he said later: "Education is the key to unlock the golden door of freedom to our people." Despite this bold vision, in 1910, Booker T. Washington moved him into a research post.

Designing the Solution

From 1914, Carver focused his efforts on using peanuts and soybeans to improve the soil, largely because they grew so well in Alabama. For more than a decade, his tests on the Tuskegee experimental farm had shown that these crops helped return nutrients to the soil, thus making it a richer growing medium. Moreover, they were important crops in their own right; peanuts and soy, both high in protein that is essential for people's diets, provided protein less expensively than meat. He summarized his ideas in 1916, in a pamphlet called *How to Grow the Peanut and 105 Ways of Preparing It for Human Consumption.*

Although growing peanuts and soybeans sounded like a perfect solution, these crops had a drawback. When farmers took Carver's advice and began growing them, the farmers discovered that no one wanted to buy them. Undeterred, Carver began the work that made him famous: he decided to expand the market for the peanut and other crops by inventing as many practical ways of using them as he could.

Over the next few decades, Carver developed hundreds of new products that used plants—mostly foods, but also inks, plastics, cosmetics, and other items. He promoted an estimated 287 products made from peanuts alone and another 118 made from sweet potatoes, although he did not invent them all himself. Carver soon became the national champion of these plants, extolling their virtues in public lectures nationwide. In 1921, for example, he lectured a congressional committee on the many beneficial uses of peanuts.

Some modern critics have suggested that Carver was more of a publicist than a scientist and more of a developer than an inventor. They argue that Carver's work played only a small part in the growth of the peanut industry; peanut growing had started to increase rapidly in the South from the late 1880s onward, years before Carver began his work. Moreover, they claim, his educational pamphlets were of limited use to illiterate farmers who could neither read nor understand them. Even after Carver's celebrated promotion of new uses for the peanut, virtually the entire crop continued to be used for peanut butter and other foodstuffs. Most of his imaginative products remained little more than amusing curiosities because the items he suggested for manufacture from peanuts or other plants could be made much more easily from other materials. Another serious charge was that he failed to document his experiments or the formulas for his work and did not publish his results in scientific journals.

Applying the Solution

Nevertheless, Carver's work won him international recognition. In 1916, he was elected a Fellow of the Royal Society of Arts of London, England. Seven years later, the National Association for the Advancement of Colored People (NAACP) presented him with a medal for his work in agriculture. In 1935, his expertise was recognized when he was appointed to an advisory role with the US Department of Agriculture. Five years later, his life became the subject of a feature film, *George Washington Carver.*

As Carver's reputation grew, he attracted the attention of many famous and influential people. The industrialist Henry Ford became a friend; Ford even built a laboratory where they worked together to devise new products. Their inventions included a new kind of rubber, a type of vehicle fuel made from soybeans, and a dent-proof plastic, made from soy, that is still being used. One of Ford's other famous friends, the inventor Thomas Edison, offered Carver a salary of $100,000 to work for him—but Carver could not be tempted away from Tuskegee.

Carver was also courted by world leaders who saw the tremendous value of his work. Three presidents—Theodore Roosevelt, Calvin Coolidge, and Franklin D. Roosevelt—traveled to Tuskegee especially to meet him. The crown prince of Sweden and Indian leader Mahatma Gandhi also sought his advice. Joseph Stalin, the leader of the Soviet Union (the former name for Russia and its nearby republics), tried to persuade Carver to move to Russia to help improve that country's cotton crop, but Carver declined this offer also.

The Impact of the Solution on Society

In 1940, Carver decided to give his life savings of $33,000 (around $558,000 US in 2014) to the Tuskegee Institute. The money was used to establish the George Washington Carver Foundation, which he hoped would continue his important agricultural research after his death. Despite his huge number of inventions and the economic importance of his work, this was a relatively modest sum. Carver had never believed in profiting from his discoveries and inventions. He said later, "One reason I never patent my products is that if I did it would take so much time, I would get nothing else done. But mainly I don't want my discoveries to benefit specific favored persons."

During World War II, when chemicals from Europe were in short supply, Carver's work took on a new significance. He helped to invent substitutes for textile dyes and, using plants, devised more than five hundred different dye colors. This was his last important work.

On January 5, 1943, at age seventy-nine, he died following a fall down a flight of stairs. The simple but moving moral of his life was inscribed on his tombstone: "He could have added fortune to fame, but caring for neither, he found happiness and honor in being helpful to the world." Soon after Carver's death, President Franklin D. Roosevelt recognized the impact of his life by dedicating the George Washington Carver National Monument, the first US national monument to an African American.

Carver's achievements earned him many honors and awards, and he was courted by famous businesspeople and the leaders of nations. Some say his achievements can also be measured in economic terms. In 1896, the peanut was not even a recognized crop in the United States. At the time of Carver's death, almost five decades later, it was one of the six leading crops in the country and second only to

George Washington Carver cultivated peanuts (a crop of which is shown here) and other produce to improve the soil.

cotton in the South. By the mid-1940s, the peanut industry that Carver championed was worth more than $200 million.

It is clear that the man who started out with so little, and with little hope of surviving into his twenties let alone fifty years after that, had great influence on the world. George Washington Carver is a name still studied and uplifted today. Without his contributions, the world would be a very different place.

Timeline

ca. 1865
George Washington Carver born near Diamond, Missouri

1890
Carver enrolls at Simpson College in Iowa

1896
Carver earns a master's degree in agricultural science and becomes director of the Department of Agricultural Research at the Tuskegee Institute

1916
Carver publishes *How to Grow the Peanut and 105 Ways of Preparing It for Human Consumption*

1921
Carver addresses a congressional committee on the many uses of peanuts

1935
Carver becomes an adviser to the US Department of Agriculture

1940
Carver donates his life savings to the Tuskegee Institute

1943
Carver dies

John Deere

1804–1886

Over the years, the agricultural industry has seen many changes. Some of these changes have greatly influenced farming trends today. They have improved the lifestyles of many individuals and continue to have significance today. Such is the case with John Deere, whose invention of the steel plow improved the lives of farmers, particularly in the Midwest. "John Deere" remains a well-known name in agriculture, but it was the original John Deere who made such a legacy possible.

Starting Out

John Deere was born February 7, 1804, in Rutland, Vermont. His father, William Rinold Deere, had emigrated from England; his

John Deere

mother, Sarah Yates, was born in Connecticut. When John was four years old, his father was lost at sea. His mother was left to raise John and his five siblings in circumstances verging on poverty.

Deere received only a basic education, attending local schools while working to assist his family financially. At age seventeen Deere began an apprenticeship to a blacksmith. He spent four years as apprentice to Captain Benjamin Lawrence in Middlebury, Vermont, before setting up shop as an independent blacksmith. Deere, who worked at this trade for the next twelve years at various locations throughout Vermont, made a good name for himself, as he was devoted to the highest-quality standards in whatever he worked on—from shoeing horses to producing household and farm implements ranging from skillets to hay rakes.

Deere married Demarius Lamb in 1827. The family moved around in central Vermont as John sought steady work, and their financial circumstances remained difficult. In 1837, with four children and another on the way, the thirty-three-year-old Deere decided to move to Illinois. He planned to establish some kind of business in the newly opened western regions of Ohio, Indiana, and Illinois, and then to send for his family once he was established. He sold his blacksmith shop in Vermont, and with about $70 in his pocket, he began the journey to Grand Detour, Illinois—a location on the Rock River where a former employer of Deere's had settled. While back in Vermont to retrieve his own family, this man had told Deere that the prairie offered great opportunity.

Defining the Problem

Eventually, Deere arrived in Grand Detour, having spent several weeks traveling by boat and by land. He quickly set up a small blacksmith shop on a rented plot. Soon he was getting work from farmers and other settlers in the area. Many of these men hailed originally from Deere's native New England, where they had learned to till the relatively light, sandy soil characteristic of that region. Out on the western prairie, the tools—particularly the plows—they had brought with them proved unequal to the very different soil they found there. These plows, made of cast iron and constructed at a poor angle for handling heavy soils, easily became clogged. Farmers complained that they had to stop every few feet to knock clods of sticky soil off their plows by hand. After hearing many such complaints, John Deere began to work on making a plow more suitable for the land.

Designing the Solution

In 1837, still in his first year in Grand Detour, Deere came up with a solution. Using a broken steel saw blade, Deere fashioned a plow that effectively cut through the soil without becoming clogged. Its highly polished surface was self-cleaning, and the plow itself literally sang through the earth: Deere's plow would eventually become known as the "singing plow" because of the unique, high-pitched sound it made as it cut neatly through the soil.

Soon his family joined him in Illinois, and Deere began to build his reputation as a plow maker, even though he could produce only a few plows a year at first because of his limited resources. Having introduced the steel plow, Deere was always concerned that someone else would come along and produce a better one. Thus he was constantly trying to improve his design—sometimes over the objections of his employees, who complained that changing the design so frequently made their work more difficult. Yet Deere insisted on making improvements whenever he had the means to do so.

The kind of steel Deere wanted could be found only in England. Transported across the Atlantic and then shipped up the Mississippi

River to the Illinois River, these special rolls of steel were costly. In response, Deere made two important moves. First, in 1848, he moved his business and his family to Moline, Illinois, on the Mississippi River, in order to take advantage of the improved transportation and waterpower that the great river offered. Second, he negotiated with a steel mill in Pittsburgh, Pennsylvania, to produce the specific steel he required. Soon he was manufacturing more than 1,500 plows a year.

Applying the Solution

As more and more farmers heard of Deere's singing plow, demand increased. Plows were shipped by boat up and down the Mississippi River and by wagon into the countryside. Many of them were taken west by settlers hoping to tame their portion of the vast territory beyond the Mississippi. By 1857, Deere's company was producing ten thousand plows a year.

> "I will never put my name on a product that does not have in it the best that is in me."
> —John Deere

John Deere's oldest surviving son, Charles, began working at the company in 1853. In the wake of the nationwide financial crisis of 1857, John Deere incorporated the company and brought his son into partnership. Having worked in positions from bookkeeper through various marketing and sales posts, Charles Deere proved to be an extremely capable businessman. The company was reincorporated as Deere and Company in 1868. Although John Deere would remain president of the company until his death in 1886, Charles ran the day-to-day operations from 1858 onward.

After 1858, John Deere's involvement in the company he had founded focused on product development and sales. He also began to give more of his time to social and philanthropic causes, eventually entering local politics. He served in a variety of civic roles in Moline before becoming mayor in 1873. Until his death there on May 17, 1886, at the age of eighty-two, John Deere contributed generously to local institutions and causes. He was widely mourned at his death.

Deere's Most Recognizable Product

Although his name is synonymous with farm and lawn tractors, John Deere did not invent the John Deere tractor associated with his name. Neither did his son Charles. Under Charles, Deere and Company expanded its product line from the steel plow to a wide range of farm implements—cultivators, planters, and many others—but it still had no connection with tractors.

In fact, Deere and Company entered the tractor business only in 1918, when, under the company's third president, William Butterworth, it acquired the Waterloo Gasoline Traction Engine Company of Waterloo, Iowa—producers of the Waterloo Boy tractor. This move, coming after several other acquisitions of farm equipment companies beginning in 1911, reinforced Deere and Company's position as a dominant American farm manufacturer. After continuing to produce and market the Waterloo Boy for several years, in 1923 Deere and Company introduced its first tractor bearing the John Deere name: the classic Model D would be produced until 1953.

Many farmers have used John Deere tractors since their introduction in 1923.

The Impact of the Solution on Society

John Deere was one of a few people who truly opened up the West to expansion. His singing plow was an indispensable tool for farmers in the untamed new lands.

Today the company still operates. John Deere remains headquartered in Moline, Illinois, where its founder established it. Its range of products spans much farther than John Deere or his son could have imagined. Its most well-known products include tractors and lawn mowers. There is little doubt that John Deere helped modernize farming with the introduction of his singing plow in 1837. His achievements will always be appreciated and celebrated, and his name will remain alive in the folds of history.

Timeline

1804
Deere born in Rutland, Vermont

1825
Deere sets up shop as a blacksmith

1837
Deere invents the "singing plow"

1857
Deere's company produces ten thousand plows per year

1858
Deere's son, Charles, takes over the day-to-day operations of the company

1873
Deere becomes mayor of Moline, Illinois

1886
Deere dies

Robert T. Fraley, Mary-Dell Chilton, and Marc Van Montagu

1953–;
1939–;
and
1933–

Genetically modified crops (or genetically modified organisms—GMOs for short) have received a great deal of attention in the press, causing debate. Some people argue that GMOs are harmful, while others attest that they can have positive effects. For instance, genetically modified plants can be disease-resistant and insect-resistant, eliminating the need for pesticides, which themselves can harm people and the environment. Genetically modified crops can also have a higher nutritional value and are hardier, which can help crops survive during years of unfavorable weather conditions. Furthermore, using genetically modified crops can increase yield, which scientists say will help the farming industry meet increasing worldwide demand for greater food production.

To understand the significance of and debate over genetically modified crops, it's important to know what they are. The term "genetically modified" refers to something with altered genetic material. In the case of crops, this means the genes of one crop have been taken and placed into another crop, altering the crop's ultimate genetic makeup. Two United States crops that are heavily impacted by genetic modification are soybeans and corn; specifically, the US Department of Agriculture reported in 2012 that 93 percent of US-grown soybeans and 88 percent of US-grown corn were genetically modified. **Canola**, developed in Canada and used in canola oil, is also genetically modified, with 97.5 percent of Canada's canola crop being genetically modified in 2012. Wheat is also often genetically modified. Because soybeans, corn, wheat, and canola are ingredients in many other products, numerous products on US grocery store shelves are genetically modified. A further concern is that genetically modified crops are often used to feed livestock, and the meat and dairy products people buy can be affected by the animals' genetically modified diet.

At the very top of this controversy are three individuals whose pioneering work in plant biotechnology led to the use of genetically modified crops: Dr. Robert T. Fraley, executive vice president and chief technology officer at sustainable-agriculture giant Monsanto; Dr. Mary-Dell Chilton, founder and researcher at Syngenta Bio-technology; and Dr. Marc Van Montagu, founder and chairman of the Institute of Plant Biotechnology Outreach at Ghent University.

The Three Major Players

Only child Dr. Marc Van Montagu was born in Ghent, Belgium, in 1933 and grew up during World War II amidst food rationing and hardship. He ultimately earned his PhD in organic chemistry and biochemistry from Ghent University. He was a director of the genetics departments at Ghent University and the Flanders Interuniversity Institute for Biotechnology, both in Belgium. He was a founder of two Belgian biotech companies—Plant Genetic Systems Inc. and CropDesign—and he is the president of the European Federation of Biotechnology and the Public Research and Regulation Initiative.

Robert T. Fraley (*left*), Mary-Dell Chilton (*middle*), and Marc Van Montagu (*right*) are pioneers in the science of genetically modified organisms.

Some of Van Montagu's pioneering work has involved research on genetic transfer using the bacteria *Agrobacterium*, as well as research on insect- and herbicide-resistant transgenic crops. For his work, Van Montagu has received numerous awards and accolades, including six honorary doctorate degrees and, in 1990, the title of baron from the king of Belgium. In 2000, he founded the Institute of Plant Biotechnology Outreach, designed to help developing countries gain access to the latest plant biotechnology research and technologies.

Dr. Mary-Dell Chilton was born in 1939 in Indianapolis, Indiana. She is a graduate of the University of Illinois, earning both her bachelor's degree and her PhD in chemistry. Chilton was fascinated by developments in DNA research during her time as a student, and she focused her doctoral thesis on how DNA can repair a cell. She completed her postdoctoral work at the University of Washington in Seattle and later taught at Washington University in St. Louis while performing research that led to the first transgenic plants.

In the late 1970s, building on the research of Van Montagu, Chilton led a research team that demonstrated that the bacteria *Agrobacterium* could be used to genetically modify plant DNA without adverse affect, resulting in disease- and pest-resistant crops. Interestingly, Chilton's groundbreaking discovery was a complete accident; one of her students had suggested in a paper that a bacteria was transferring its DNA to plants, and Chilton found the theory intriguing but utter nonsense. She joined the research team to try to disprove the theory—and was delighted to ultimately be proven wrong. The research cemented her career in a male-driven field.

Chilton's work led her to be referred to as the "queen of *Agrobacterium*" and to receive an honorary doctorate from the University of Louvain in Belgium. In addition to numerous awards and accolades, Chilton was inducted into the National Inventors Hall of Fame in 2015.

Dr. Robert T. Fraley was born in 1953 and grew up on a grain and livestock farm in Illinois. Like Mary-Dell Chilton, he earned his bachelor's degree as well as a PhD in microbiology and biochemistry from the University of Illinois. He completed his postdoctoral research in biophysics at the University of California–San Francisco. Fraley started at agricultural giant Monsanto in 1981, working as a molecular biologist. His early research at Monsanto built upon the research of both Van Montagu and Chilton. Fraley quickly moved up at Monsanto with his self-confident and ambitious visions for the company. Among numerous other prizes and accolades, in 1999 he was awarded the National Medal of Technology by then-president Bill Clinton.

Together with Chilton and Van Montagu, Fraley received the World Food Prize in 2013 for his pioneering work in genetically modified crops.

Defining the Problem

Before genetically modified crops were introduced in the 1980s, traditional farming methods produced corn, soybeans, and canola in the US and other countries. However, the crops were susceptible to inclement weather and to insects, which sometimes made it difficult to meet food-production demands. With food-production demands expected to steadily increase in future years, it was clear that a solution was needed.

Designing the Solution

The idea of selective breeding in agriculture is nothing new—farmers have been doing it for thousands of years. However, the process is slow and has limited possible combinations. Genetic modification accomplishes the same goal—a stronger, more sustainable end product—but does so much more quickly. By "cutting and pasting" traits from one crop to another, scientists can quickly accomplish a process that takes many generations to happen through selective breeding.

Robert T. Fraley, Mary-Dell Chilton, and Marc Van Montagu worked independently on finding plant biotechnology solutions that would strengthen crops and increase yield. Chilton and Van Montagu both worked on technology that would enable food scientists to transfer foreign genes into plants. This discovery allowed scientists to create disease-resistant plants that could withstand extreme weather conditions, such as drought and extreme heat, as well as fight off insects. Building upon their pioneering work, Fraley focused on soybeans, attempting to transfer immunity to specific bacteria into plants.

The three scientists shared their research at the 1983 Miami Winter Biochemistry Symposium, changing the face of agricultural practices. The race was on to use this new technology to improve crops and increase yield.

Applying the Solution

Although the first known genetically modified food item was a tomato, introduced in the United States in 1994, a major development in genetically modified crops was introduced in 1996, when Robert T. Fraley developed the first herbicide-resistant soybean, which was significant because it allowed farmers to spray herbicides such as Roundup on their fields without killing their soybean crops in the process. Now, herbicide-resistant crops are the most widely grown genetically modified crops; 70 percent of genetically modified crops grown worldwide are herbicide-resistant.

In the years since Fraley's introduction of the herbicide-resistant soybean, says the International Service for the Acquisition of Agri-biotech Applications, 17.3 million farmers in nearly thirty countries worldwide have taken to growing genetically enhanced crops on more than 420 million acres (170 million ha) of farmland, mostly in developing countries but also in the United States and Canada. Most of these farmers have small farms and limited resources, so making use of genetically engineered crops to ensure a decent harvest is of the utmost importance to them.

The Impact of the Solution on Society

Genetically modified crops have had a massive impact on society, both negatively and positively. Farmers are pleased to have stronger, more resilient crops that result in a better overall yield. However, the public is concerned about the long-term impact of genetically modifying the substances that people put in their bodies, saying that the long-term health effects of consuming genetically altered foods are unknown, as are the long-term environmental impacts.

On an environmental level, organic farmers have expressed concern that due to the potential for **cross-pollination**, genetically modified crops could contaminate traditional crops as well as **biopharmed** crops used in pharmaceuticals such as vaccines. Further, cross-pollination could create problems if certain genetically modified crops unsafe for human consumption (such as certain strains of corn) are planted near crops meant for human consumption. Organic food advocates have cited that not enough research has been done to ensure the safety of long-term consumption of modified foods.

Many plant biotechnologists, including Chilton and Van Montagu, have argued against concerns of long-term risk, saying that no risks from consuming and using genetically modified crops have been identified, and that the crops are heavily tested before being put into use, so any potentially negative impacts would have been caught during the testing process.

Whether genetically modified crops are a positive or a negative, technological development has been heavily debated and inspires passionate responses from people on both sides of the argument. However, in 2013, the nonprofit World Food Prize Foundation refused to allow its decision to be tainted by the controversy

In Hawaii, a woman working for a GMO company places a pollination bag over a corn tassel in an attempt to cross-pollinate.

surrounding genetically modified foods, and it awarded the prize to Fraley, Chilton, and Van Montagu for their pioneering work in plant biotechnology. The prize was created to recognize people who improve the quality, quantity, or availability of food. However, people who oppose the use of genetically modified crops are not happy with the decision. They worry that the prize was awarded for personal rather than scientific reasons.

Europe has strict regulations on GMOs, which are at some level banned in France, Germany, Austria, Hungary, Greece, and Luxembourg. The full impact of genetically modified crops on North American society, however, remains to be seen and depends largely on whether the United States and Canada begin to enact bans on genetically modified crops. Only time will tell what the impact of these foods on the world and humanity will be.

Timeline

1933
Marc Van Montagu born

1939
Mary-Dell Chilton born

1953
Robert Fraley born

1983
Fraley, Chilton, and Van Montagu independently share their research findings on genetically modified crops at the Miami Winter Biochemistry Symposium

1994
First genetically modified food—a tomato—is produced

1996
Fraley introduces the herbicide-resistant soybean

2000
Van Montagu founds the Institute of Plant Biotechnology Outreach

2012
For the first time, biotech crops grown in developing countries outnumber biotech crops grown in industrial countries

2013
Fraley, Chilton, and Van Montagu share the 2013 World Food Prize

Inventor of Food Preservation Methods

Lloyd A. Hall

1894–1971

As people and machines have evolved, so too have ways of making food last longer. One of the developers of methods of preserving food was Lloyd A. Hall. For much of the latter part of his life, Hall invented techniques of curing and preserving food, many of which are still used today. He was a significant person in the history of food as we know it today.

The Inventor Grows Up

Lloyd Augustus Hall was born in Elgin, Illinois, on June 20, 1894. In the 1830s his paternal grandfather had been a founding member, and later pastor, of the Quinn Chapel A.M.E. Church—the first African-American church in Chicago. His maternal grandmother

Lloyd Hall pursued a chemistry degree at Northwestern University
(pictured here ca. 1907).

had come to the city at about the same time via the **Underground
Railroad**. Hall's father, Augustus Hall, also became a minister in a
Chicago Baptist church. Both his father and his mother, Isabel, had
graduated from high school in the Chicago area.

The family lived in nearby Aurora, where Lloyd Hall attended East
Side High School. Active in athletics and captain of the debate team,
he graduated near the top of his class and was offered scholarships to
several universities in Illinois. He selected Northwestern University
in Evanston, just north of Chicago. As a chemistry student there,
he befriended a fellow student, Carroll L. Griffith, whose family
would later found Griffith Laboratories. That association would later
play a very important role in Hall's career. After graduating from
Northwestern in 1916, he began taking graduate courses in chemistry
at the University of Chicago.

Hall took a job in the laboratories of the Chicago Department
of Health in 1917 and quickly became a senior chemist. He also
served briefly during World War I, inspecting explosives in an
ordnance department in Wisconsin. Hall worked in various industrial
concerns for a number of years before he joined the Boyer Chemical
Laboratory in Chicago as a chief chemist in 1921. At Boyer, Hall first
developed his interest in the emerging field of food chemistry. One
year later, he took a job as president of a consulting lab in Chicago.
He worked as an independent consultant for the next several years.

Defining the Problem

In 1924, Carroll Griffith offered Hall the use of his laboratories while Hall carried out his consulting work. What began as an informal arrangement soon turned into the most lasting and valuable association in Hall's career. In 1925, Hall became director of research at Griffith as well as the company's chief chemist. He continued independent consulting until 1929, when he devoted himself full-time to Griffith Laboratories. He remained with the company until his retirement in 1959.

Griffith Laboratories was one of the pioneers in bringing scientific innovation to the food industry. Lloyd Hall, already interested in improving the foods available to consumers, found an ideal environment at Griffith for carrying out his research. Although he was involved in many of Griffith's important projects, Hall is remembered chiefly for three major improvements for which he is responsible: creating a type of sodium crystal for preserving meats; sterilizing spices; and preventing rancidity, or spoiling, in fats and oils.

Designing the Solution

Hall's first major contribution to food preservation came with improving the existing method of preserving and curing meats. Using a "flash-drying" approach, he developed a kind of crystal compound, made of common table salt and sodium nitrate, that allowed the salt to penetrate the meat, thus preserving it, while the nitrates acted to further cure the meat, maintaining its original color and texture (see sidebar, The Problem with Meats).

Applying the Solution

Hall's advances in meat preservation quickly caught on in the food industry. With Hall at the helm of research, Griffith Laboratories gained a wider reputation as a leader in food chemistry. Other major advances soon followed.

In addition to meat-curing crystals, Hall created a process for sterilizing spices, thus ridding them of any contaminants. All kinds of dried spices, as well as dried vegetables such as onion powder, were subject to attack by various bacteria and yeasts, and their shelf life was, accordingly, fairly short. No satisfactory means of ridding these spices of impurities without ruining their taste and appearance had yet been found.

Hall experimented with various approaches, including heat-drying spices in the air and baking them in an oven, but none proved effective while also maintaining flavor and color. He finally arrived at a solution by using a kind of gas, ethylene oxide, to kill the contaminants and germs in spices. He placed spices in a vacuum chamber to remove their moisture and allow the gas to enter the

The Problem with Meats

Soon after joining Griffith, Hall sought a better way to preserve and cure meats. The most common way of preserving up to this time (the mid-1920s) was to use sodium chloride—common table salt. Curing meats involves using chemicals, often nitrogen compounds such as nitrates or nitrites, in combination with salt to further preserve the color and appearance of salted meat. By coming up with a method of flash drying these salt and nitrogen compounds, Hall solved an old problem: how to allow the sodium chloride to penetrate the meat first to preserve it adequately, before the nitrate compounds would enter. All previous experience demonstrated that nitrates and nitrites penetrated meat faster than salt, causing the meat to disintegrate before it had been properly preserved.

Hall speculated that if nitrate compounds could be combined with salt to form a third substance, then they could penetrate the meat at a rate that would allow proper preservation and maintain the original color, appearance, and texture. He sought to achieve this combination by very quickly drying (flash drying) a solution of nitrate compounds and sodium chloride over hot metal rollers. The crystals that resulted from this evaporation consisted of a nitrate center surrounded by a salt crust. This was just the structure needed: as the crystals dissolved, the salt would penetrate the meat first. Hall's crystals quickly became the most popular meat-curing product on the market.

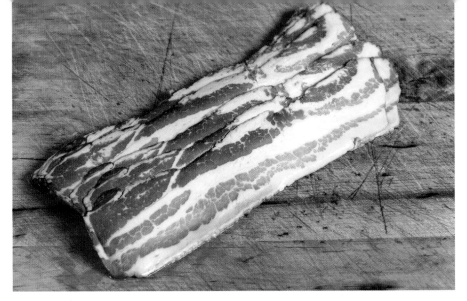

Hall developed a better way to preserve meats such as bacon.

spices. The method Hall developed to sterilize spices is still used to sterilize medical instruments and some medicines.

A third major advance Hall made in food chemistry involved the use of antioxidants to prevent fats or oils from becoming rancid, or spoiling. Fats or oils in food can become rancid when they come into contact with oxygen. Hall found that antioxidants occurring naturally in crude, unrefined vegetable oil could be mixed with salt to create a substance that would prevent fats and oils from spoiling. The antioxidants kept these fats from reacting with oxygen, thereby giving them a longer shelf life.

The Impact of the Solution on Society

Hall played an important role in many other advances within the food industry. Notable among these was his work to reduce the time for curing bacon from a couple of weeks to only a few hours, in the process improving the bacon's quality and taste. He won a patent for this invention—one among many over his career. He served on many local, state, and national boards, including the Chicago chapters of the National Association for the Advancement of Colored People (NAACP) and the Urban League (both devoted to equality for African Americans); the Illinois State Food Commission; the

Science Advisory Board on Food Research; and the Institute of Food Technologists, of which he was also a cofounder.

After he retired from Griffith Laboratories in 1959, Hall served several months in Indonesia as consultant for the United Nations' Food and Agricultural Organization unit. President John F. Kennedy appointed him in 1962 to the American Food for Peace Council, where he remained until 1964. Throughout the rest of his life, Hall served in a variety of organizations and causes in the same spirit that had led him to invent improved food preservation methods more than thirty years earlier. In his final years, Hall worked to help underprivileged young people get the training they needed to work in chemistry. Hall died on January 2, 1971, in Altadena, California, where he had moved with his wife following his retirement. Hall was inducted posthumously into the National Inventors Hall of Fame in 2004.

Today Hall is remembered as a leader of food preservation methods. His array of achievements benefited many aspects of the food industry, and many techniques he utilized continue to be practiced today.

Timeline

1894
Lloyd Hall born in Elgin, Illinois

1916
Hall graduates with chemistry degree from Northwestern University

1921
Hall joins Boyer Chemical Laboratory in Chicago

1925
Hall becomes director of research at Griffith Laboratories

1959
Hall retires from Griffith

1962
Hall works with the American Food for Peace Council

1971
Hall dies

Inventor of Vacuum Canning

Amanda Jones

1835–1914

Throughout the history of food and agriculture technology, women have played a role in inventing new and exciting products. One woman who is responsible for introducing a new way of canning food to society was Amanda Jones. This woman led an interesting life, full of challenge and controversy, and her method of canning persists even to this day. She is an example to other women that they do not have to be afraid to invent, and invent well.

Starting Out

Amanda Theodosia Jones was born in 1835 in East Bloomfield, New York, to a large family. Her father was a weaver, and the

Amanda Jones spent her young life in Buffalo, New York (pictured here).

family was not wealthy. Both of her parents were avid readers who valued education.

In 1845, Jones's family moved to a small town near Buffalo, New York. One day, Jones was attending school with one of her brothers when he suddenly collapsed and died. That experience elicited a fascination with **spiritualism** in Jones, who wanted to contact her dead brother.

Spiritualism, a religious movement that became popular in the 1840s, claimed that the spirits of the deceased could be contacted by gifted individuals known as mediums. Mediums could allegedly communicate with spirits while asleep or in a trance. Often a medium claimed to have a particular spirit guide who would speak through him or her, providing advice and insight.

In 1850, Jones graduated from a normal school, where teachers were trained, and she began teaching. She also began writing poetry. Her first poems were published in 1854. Jones then quit teaching to focus on her writing.

Defining the Problem

During the 1860s, Jones continued to publish poems and worked as an editor. She had chronic health problems, and her interest in spiritualism intensified, even leading her to believe that she herself was a medium. She eventually claimed to have been in contact with various spirit guides who would instruct her to move or take up new occupations.

"This is a woman's industry. No man will vote our stock, transact our business, pronounce on women's wages, supervise our factories. Give men whatever work is suitable, but keep the governing power."
—Amanda Jones, addressing employees of the Woman's Canning and Preserving Company

In 1872, Jones had an idea for a new way to can fruit. Canning had been invented in the early 1800s as a means of preserving food for long periods. At the time, canning involved first sealing food in a can or jar, then cooking it at high temperature for a long time. As a result, canning food was grueling, and canned food was not nearly as flavorful or nutritious as fresh food.

Jones would later claim that her spirit guides suggested that food could be canned without cooking it. Jones got the idea that food could perhaps be canned at a lower temperature if all the air was vacuumed out of the can and replaced with fruit juice or syrup.

Designing the Solution

Jones traveled to the home of a distant relative, LeRoy Cooley, living in Albany, New York. Jones and Cooley went to work developing Jones's canning idea, and in 1873, they were granted several patents for what would become known as the Jones process.

Fruit to be canned by the Jones process was placed in a jar. An air pump was then used to remove as much air as possible from the jar. Juice or syrup was then poured into the jar, which was subsequently heated, causing the fluids inside to boil. Because the air pressure was so low in the jar, boiling would occur at temperatures as low as

Jones and Spiritualism

Jones's desire to be recognized as a psychic medium and inventor created a unique conundrum about assigning credit for her ideas: her alleged contact with the spirit world and her insistence that she dutifully followed the instructions of spirits could suggest that she was using the ideas of others. The issue was particularly problematic for Jones because her spirit guides were usually male. At the time, men were considered by many to be intellectually superior to women.

This photograph seems to show a musical instrument rising into the air during a séance.

Sensitive to the possibility of being regarded as intellectually inferior, Jones detailed in her autobiography precisely how her spirit guides assisted her: they told her about patent law, that it was possible to can fruit without cooking it, and that she should work with Cooley to develop the idea.

She insisted, however, that the Jones process was her own invention, created without explicit instruction by spirits. She maintained that she woke up one day with the basic idea that later she and Cooley developed into a workable process without the benefit of otherworldly instruction. "Now, let me say at once, no spirit told me this," she wrote. "I have inventions—patentable—patented. They are as much my own as are my many poems—mostly studied out by slow and painful process, often at bitter cost. To every patent application I have taken oath, unperjured: 'This is my invention.—This I claim.'"

Inventors of Food and Agriculture Technology

100 degrees Fahrenheit (37.8 degrees Celsius). Low temperatures created an additional complication: they were not high enough to kill bacteria in food, which traditional canning, with its high temperatures, did. The process remained effective nonetheless because it deprived bacteria and molds of oxygen, which they needed to survive and grow.

Although Jones and Cooley patented their ideas, they did not attempt to turn them into a business at the time. Instead, Jones moved on to other interests.

In 1880, Jones traveled to western Pennsylvania to examine that area's oil fields. At the time, this form of oil was a relatively new fuel. People were accustomed to burning solid fuel such as coal; liquid oil tended to spill and cause fires.

Jones developed and patented an automatic safety burner, which had a valve to control the amount of oil released into the burner. Tests of the new burner helped Jones to attract a financial backer; however, the backer's fortune was lost in a stock-market collapse, leaving Jones without the funds she needed to turn her idea into a business.

Applying the Solution

In 1890, Jones returned to her vacuum-canning idea, founding the Woman's Canning and Preserving Company in Chicago. As the company's name suggested, all of the employees were women (except Cooley and the man who operated the building's boiler), as were all of its stockholders.

The company began selling canned rice and tapioca puddings, eventually moving into canned meat. Woman's Canning expanded, opening two new facilities. The company's other executives began to lose confidence in Jones's management, however, and she was forced out of the business in 1893.

The Impact of the Solution on Society

Undaunted by the loss of control over her company, Jones continued to patent improvements to her burner and the Jones process. She also continued to write, publishing her autobiography in 1910. She died in 1914, seven years before Woman's Canning went out of business.

Vacuum canning remains a standard method for foods that will lose flavor if exposed to high heat. The process has been modified over the years for use with dry foodstuffs like coffee, which is vacuum-canned and packed with nitrogen rather than juice or syrup. Jones's innovations made canning a versatile method of preserving food for longer periods with less loss of flavor and nutrition.

Jones herself is remembered as a remarkable inventor and contributor to the advance of modern food packaging and preservation. Without her, the canning process would be different and perhaps not as thorough or beneficial as it is today. Her determination to make her idea a reality, and to do it with the help of other women, is an example to others never to back down on their dreams.

Timeline

1835
Amanda Jones born in East Bloomfield, New York

1850
Jones graduates from normal school

1872
Jones develops a new canning method

1880
Jones develops an automatic safety burner

1890
Jones founds the Woman's Canning and Preserving Company

1893
Jones is forced out of her company

1914
Jones dies

Inventor of Corn Flakes

Will Keith Kellogg

1860–1951

Every morning, men, women, and children in the United States and around the world eat the first meal of the day, breakfast. Sometimes people eat toast or eggs and bacon, while others choose to eat cereal. Cereal was not always part of the breakfast options, however. It was not until the nineteenth and twentieth centuries that cereal became the popular breakfast item we know today. This was thanks to a man named Will Kellogg, who wanted to bring something different to people's eating habits. The introduction of Kellogg's Corn Flakes sparked a cereal revolution, resulting in many people eating the food for centuries to come.

Kellogg Is Born

Will Keith Kellogg was born on April 7, 1860, in Battle Creek, Michigan, the town that would become famous for its breakfast cereal industry. Kellogg was written off as "dim-witted" by his teachers, but years later he would discover that he was merely nearsighted. He left school at age fifteen and started working as a traveling salesman in his father's broom-making business.

"Dollars do not produce character."

—Will Kellogg

His older brother, John Harvey Kellogg, was a charismatic physician and a devoted Seventh-day Adventist. Like most members of that health-oriented Christian denomination, he was also a vegetarian. John Harvey Kellogg became head physician and supervisor at the Battle Creek Sanitarium, a well-known health spa and hospital that had been founded in 1866 by the Seventh-day Adventists. One of his chief aims was to improve the health of his patients through a strictly vegetarian diet. When Will was twenty years old, he went to work as his brother's assistant.

Defining the Problem

Will Kellogg became interested in nutrition while working at the sanitarium. Many of his brother John's ideas for dietary improvement were a little unusual, such as the all-grape diet, but others had more promise. The brothers began to research a variety of whole grain foods in order to provide patients with a healthy diet. They first developed a wheat flake, which all of the patients liked very much (see sidebar, The Corn Flake Arrives). The new flakes, called "Granose," became so popular that many patients asked to have packages sent to their homes after leaving the sanitarium.

Will wanted to market their new product more widely. His older brother, however, insisted that the cereal be used only for his patients. The result was that one of the sanitarium's patients, C. W. Post, tasted the wheat flakes and set out to reproduce them. He succeeded—to the point that his own cereal company, which would produce such

William Keith Kellogg (*center right*) with companions in February 1925

items as Post Toasties, would eventually become the General Foods Corporation. Other cereal makers in Battle Creek followed Post's example and began making similar wheat flakes. Between 1900 and 1905, more than forty cereal companies had begun operating there.

Will Kellogg was unhappy with his brother's lack of ambition, so when he succeeded in developing a similar kind of flake using corn instead of wheat, he determined not to miss out on the opportunity this time.

Designing the Solution

After much experimenting, he came up with what he felt was a better, crunchier, tastier flake. The brothers established Sanitas Food Company in 1898 to sell corn flakes by mail order. Although John was content to produce flakes on a small scale, serving only the sanitarium and its patients, Will had much bigger plans.

The Corn Flake Arrives

The corn flake has become the signature product of the W. K. Kellogg Company, but first came the wheat flake. The invention of the wheat flake came about one day by accident in the sanitarium where Will was assisting his brother, John Harvey Kellogg.

In an effort to create a more easily digested bread substitute for patients at the Battle Creek Sanitarium, the brothers were experimenting with boiling different grains prior to baking. One evening in 1894 or 1895, without meaning to, Will had let a pot of boiled wheat stand several hours before baking it. In the process, though Kellogg did not know this, the wheat had softened somewhat, or had become "tempered." Kellogg went ahead and rolled the wheat out and let it dry. He saw that each individual grain of wheat emerged within the mash as a thin flake. After he baked these flakes, he discovered that he had created a cereal that was very tasty, crisp, and easily eaten and digested.

The brothers served these wheat flakes, which they dubbed "Granose," to patients in the sanitarium.

Intent on turning his corn flake business into a global packaged food enterprise, in 1906 Will Kellogg established the Battle Creek Toasted Flakes Company. Kellogg aggressively promoted his company and its product, and success came quickly: in its first year, the company shipped 175,000 cases of corn flakes. Within five years, Kellogg's Corn Flakes had found their way into the majority of kitchens across America.

Applying the Solution

With corn flakes as his staple product, Kellogg soon expanded his product line, introducing Kellogg's Bran Flakes in 1915, Kellogg's All-Bran in 1916, and Kellogg's Rice Krispies in 1928. In 1922, the business was renamed the W. K. Kellogg Company. Shortly thereafter, the company began operating in Canada, Australia, Europe, and Asia. Kellogg was one of the first American entrepreneurs to recognize the vast potential of international markets. He is also credited with the invention of such marketing techniques as including product giveaways and color advertising in magazines.

Will Kellogg retired in 1929 as president of the W. K. Kellogg Company. He remained as chairman of the board until 1946. During this time he became increasingly involved with philanthropic activities. As early as 1925, he had formed the Fellowship Corporation to foster agricultural training. In 1930, he established the W. K. Kellogg Child Welfare Foundation after having been named a delegate to the White House Conference on Child Health and Protection by President Herbert Hoover. The Child Welfare Foundation then became the W. K. Kellogg Foundation. It remains one of the leading charitable institutions in the United States, donating more than $4.5 billion between 1930 and 2006. The foundation has continued to focus on children's welfare; Kellogg strongly supported educating children and giving them the means to achieve independence and security because he believed the future of humanity depended upon it.

Kellogg spent his last years living mostly in California. He owned a horse ranch in Pomona and left this property to California State Polytechnic College for use as a campus. He was opposed to leaving

Today, the Kellogg headquarters are still based in Battle Creek, Michigan.

his wealth to his children for fear that doing so would stifle their own ambition and independence. Kellogg died in Battle Creek on October 6, 1951.

The Impact of the Solution on Society

Kellogg is a name that will go down in history as a significant inventor of breakfast items. Today his company spans many products. Among the most famous Kellogg brands are Keebler, Pop-Tarts, Cheez-It, Morningstar Farms, Famous Amos, and Eggo.

Kellogg not only brought society a different take to breakfast but also improved the industry around Battle Creek. Today Battle Creek remains the area where Kellogg's is headquartered. In addition to his effects on local industry, Kellogg's ambition led him to establish the W. K. Kellogg Foundation. This organization still exists today and works to promote projects relating to health, agriculture, and education to help people around the world achieve independence. Kellogg's impact on society is immense, and the cereals he and his company established remain important parts of people's daily morning meal.

Timeline

1860
Will Keith Kellogg born in Battle Creek, Michigan

1875
Kellogg leaves school to work as a traveling salesman

1880
Kellogg works as an assistant to his brother John

1898
The Kellogg brothers establish the Sanitas Food Company to sell their new corn flakes

1906
Will Kellogg establishes the Battle Creek Toasted Flakes Company

1922
Kellogg renames his company the W. K. Kellogg Company

1915–1928
Bran Flakes, All-Bran, and Rice Krispies are introduced to the market

1946
Kellogg retires as chairman of the board of the Kellogg Company

1951
Kellogg dies

Inventor of the Mechanical Reaper

Cyrus Hall McCormick

1809–1884

At the beginning of the nineteenth century, farming was a popular profession for nearly 90 percent of people living in the United States. It was this industry that helped shape America into the country it is today. Various mechanisms were responsible for making farming so popular in the nineteenth century and contributed to continuing the profession today in the United States. One of the most important advances in agricultural devices was the mechanical reaper by Cyrus McCormick. This invention influenced the way farming was practiced and helped open the United States to more opportunities out west. Overall, it inspired the creation of other similar devices, all of which impacted the United States as a whole and helped shape modern society.

Cyrus Hall McCormick

Dawn on the Inventor

Cyrus McCormick's family had been farmers for several generations.
His grandfather, Robert McCormick, had settled on a large farm in
Rockbridge County, Virginia, in the Shenandoah Valley near the
Blue Ridge Mountains, in 1779. Farming and milling made Robert
McCormick wealthy; he built a manor house on his land and furnished
it expensively. Robert had five children, one of whom, born in 1780,
was named Robert Jr. The younger Robert acquired a nearby farm,
Walnut Grove, and his eldest son, Cyrus Hall McCormick, was born
there on February 15, 1809.

Defining the Problem

Robert McCormick Jr. was a blacksmith and inventor as well as a farmer. At the time, most farming jobs were done by hand. During harvest time, many extra laborers had to be hired at considerable expense. McCormick realized he would make more money if he could invent machines to help him gather crops from his fields. He may have been aware of a British reaping machine patented in 1800 by Joseph Boyce or perhaps the idea occurred to him independently. Around 1815, Robert McCormick began to experiment with a horse-drawn reaper. His idea was that the machine would chop and collect grain as a horse dragged it through the fields. Robert McCormick worked on this invention for years but never made it function to his satisfaction. Each year at harvest time, he tinkered with the machine and tried to get it to work; each year he ended up harvesting his grain the traditional way, with scythes (curved blades on long wooden handles that workers swung back and forth through the crops).

Inspired by his father, Cyrus tried his hand at inventing, too. Like many children of this period, he had little education at school. Instead, he helped on the farm and watched his father tinkering in his foundry and workshop. In 1824, at fifteen years of age, he invented a new kind of **cradle** that could be used to cut and stack grain more efficiently. Six years later, he developed two new plows. In 1831, his father gave up his plan to make a reaper after struggling with it for more than fifteen years. However, Cyrus was not content to let a promising invention die. When he examined his father's designs, he was certain he could make them work.

Designing the Solution

In early 1831, at age twenty-two, he built a reaping machine that actually worked. The idea was simple: two horses would drag the machine through the fields of grain. As the reaper passed over the tall growing stalks, a revolving reel grabbed the grain and pulled it backward. A blade, moving back and forth, cut the heads of grain from the stalks and collected them on a large platform at the back, ready for milling.

By July 1831, the reaper was ready for its first public test. A large crowd gathered to watch as young Cyrus McCormick wheeled out his machine. It made a great deal of noise and scared the horses that were pulling it. Nevertheless, it cut the grain far more quickly than laborers could. Using the McCormick reaper, two men (one guiding the horses and one operating the reaper) could harvest 40 acres (16 ha) of grain in one day; eight men with scythes would be needed to cut that amount in the same time.

Despite this success, McCormick initially did little with his invention. He patented it in 1834 but did not manufacture or sell it to others. Following the financial panic of 1837 (a national stock market crash and depression), the McCormicks found themselves deeply in debt, and Cyrus realized that his invention could help them. In the following few years, he made small numbers of reapers in the family foundry. In 1840 and 1841, he sold two reapers, but production grew rapidly. Just three years later, he made and sold fifty.

In 1844, McCormick started traveling around the Midwest, seeking orders for his new business. This trip convinced him that the demand for reaping machines was huge, and he decided to start making them in greater numbers. In 1847, he relocated to Chicago, then a small town, which was closer to the country's agricultural heartland. He interested Chicago's mayor, William Ogden, in the project and the two became partners. Soon, they had established a giant factory, which used a novel manufacturing method of mass production (in which many machines are made simultaneously instead of one at a time) to reduce costs and increase profit. In the factory's first year of operation, McCormick and Ogden made and sold eight hundred reapers. In a few years, McCormick was a household name throughout the nation. Within a decade, his company was the biggest maker of farm machinery in the United States.

Applying the Solution

In 1848, the patent on McCormick's reaper expired and his rivals fought a legal battle that stopped him from renewing it. Because anyone was now free to copy his invention, McCormick was forced to market his machine much more aggressively just to survive. He adopted some novel sales techniques to win over customers. McCormick pioneered the idea of buying on credit: instead of having to save the money to pay cash for their machines, farmers could take immediate delivery and pay over time with the money they saved on hired laborers. McCormick's company was one of the first to use advertisements with **testimonials**. He also hired traveling salesmen who took the reaper out to demonstrate it to farmers on their own land. To reassure customers further, every machine carried a warranty.

Not content with revolutionizing agriculture in the United States, McCormick was soon selling his machine around the world. In 1851, he demonstrated it at the world's fair in London, England—a showcase for all the latest inventions and technologies—where the reaper won the grand prize. Four years later, it won a similar prize at an exhibition in Paris, France. The resulting publicity helped McCormick's reaper to spread rapidly through Europe.

A Reaper Rival

More than one hundred years after the death of Cyrus Hall McCormick, people still celebrate a man whose invention revolutionized agriculture. Fewer remember Obed Hussey (1792–1860), who developed a rival reaping machine around the same time. Born in Maine, Hussey later moved to Cincinnati, Ohio, where he developed his invention in the early 1830s. Hussey patented his machine on December 31, 1833, six months before McCormick's own patent was filed, though McCormick had apparently invented his machine first.

Unlike McCormick, Hussey started selling his machines immediately. McCormick claimed that Hussey had copied his machine, and a bitter rivalry developed. McCormick wrote letters to the press to "inform Mr. Hussey ... and warn all persons against the use of" his ideas. Hussey was undeterred. In 1843, he challenged McCormick to a reaping test near Richmond. Afterward, the local newspaper reported: "The committee feel great reluctance in deciding between them. But, upon the whole, prefer McCormick's."

McCormick was soon selling thousands of machines every year. He kept releasing improved versions of his reaper every few years, both to keep his customers interested and so he could take out new patents. In the 1850s, for example, he developed machines that had seats for the driver and the reaper operator and cut a bigger width of crop than the original 1831 machine. In 1858, he made a machine called the Self-Rake Reaper (also known as "Old Reliable") that was more efficient in several ways. It did away with the horse driver entirely: one person sitting on the reaper at the back could now control both the horses and the reaping machine. Also, an automatic rake on the back platform swept the cut grain into neat piles on the ground that could be bundled up easily by a following machine. McCormick developed many more machines in the years that followed.

The Impact of the Solution on Society

Now established as a hugely successful businessman, McCormick began to explore other avenues. He became active in politics,

In 1848, McCormick's patent expired after its original fifteen-year term. When he tried to renew it, Hussey fought him in court, and McCormick lost the case. However, the battle between the two inventors continued. Hussey took his machines to Britain in 1851, the same year McCormick crossed the Atlantic, and even sold two of his reapers to Queen Victoria's husband, Prince Albert. However, as McCormick stepped up production, Hussey was driven out of business and his name faded into obscurity.

In 1912, the writer Follett L. Greeno tried to set the record straight (as he saw it). In *Obed Hussey, Who, of All Inventors, Made Bread Cheap*, Greeno heaped praise upon the forgotten inventor: "Obed Hussey is dead, but his machine still lives, an article of measureless value to the great world of agriculture." According to Greeno, Hussey was "a natural inventor" who was too "sensitive, modest, and unassuming" to fight for his rightful place in history.

supporting the Democratic Party, and in the Presbyterian Church, helping to establish a seminary in Chicago. He became one of Chicago's most distinguished citizens and edited the *Chicago Times* until 1861. Disaster struck McCormick in 1871 when a fire gutted his factory. By this time, however, the worldwide success of his reaper had made him extremely wealthy, and he simply rebuilt. He also began to invest some of his fortune in railroads and mines. In 1879, he renamed his firm the McCormick Harvesting Machine Company; he served as its president until his death at age seventy-five, on May 13, 1884.

The McCormick Company's success continued throughout the 1880s and 1890s, with McCormick's son, Cyrus McCormick Jr. (1859–1936), installed as president. The competition grew tougher, however, and in 1900, the company merged with its rival, Deering Harvester, to form the International Harvester Company. In 1984, International merged with the Case Corporation, which still owns the McCormick name. The McCormick farm at Raphine is now an experimental farm run by Virginia Polytechnic Institute and State University and maintains some of McCormick's original equipment as a working museum.

McCormick's invention helped change the face of agriculture, both in the United States and in the wider world. Because of the success of McCormick's reaper, and the many rival machines that it inspired, crops could be harvested with a fraction of the labor that was previously needed. People were freed from the farms; many moved to towns and cities to work in factories. The reaper also reduced the need for additional workers at harvest, so it played a part in the decline of slavery from the mid-nineteenth century. During the American Civil War, many agricultural workers went to fight, and labor shortages on farms became acute. This proved fortunate for McCormick and his rivals: between 1860 and 1865, the number of mechanical reapers on farms almost tripled, from around 90,000 to 250,000.

Using McCormick's reaper, farmers could harvest more crops more quickly than ever before, and many doubled their landholdings and acreage planted. As the United States expanded westward into

A modern harvester at work

new territories, the McCormick reaper helped farmers put newly acquired land into agricultural production. When railroads were laid into the newly opened territories, they helped to create and maintain vast new markets for the company's enthusiastic sales force. Thus expansion of the United States and sales of the reaper drove each other forward in tandem. It was once said that McCormick's machine helped push the boundary of the United States 30 miles (64 km) farther west every year.

The McCormick Company made use of this idea for decades. Early advertisements featured a famous painting, Emmanuel Leutze's mural *Westward the Course of Empire Takes Its Way* (1860), which shows pioneer settlers heading west for a new land of promise. In the advertisement, the title became *Westward the Course of Empire Takes Its Way with McCormick Reapers in the Van*. In the 1930s, the International Harvester Company advertised its diesel-powered trucks as modern versions of the covered wagons used by pioneers.

Although McCormick owed much of his success to a simple and effective invention, the way he marketed his machine was equally important. Persuasive advertising and sales techniques helped to convince farmers that they could not manage without a McCormick reaper. As more and more farmers bought mechanical reapers, skeptical farmers quickly found themselves in a minority. By proving the worth of mechanized agriculture, McCormick helped to bring about an entirely new era in history: growing and harvesting food was no longer humankind's chief occupation.

Today the McCormick name lives on in the pages of agricultural history. His invention, although not without competition, changed the way many farmers around the country conquered large fields and harvested their crops. Without this invention, modern farming techniques would be missing one of their most essential parts.

Timeline

1809
Cyrus McCormick born in Virginia

1831
McCormick invents
reaping machine

1844
McCormick travels the Midwest,
taking orders for his reaper

1847
McCormick relocates to Chicago
and opens a factory

1848
McCormick's patent expires

1851
McCormick displays his
reaping machine at the
world's fair in London

1858
McCormick builds the
Self-Rake Reaper

1871
A fire destroys
McCormick's factory

1879
McCormick's company is
renamed the McCormick
Harvesting Machine Company

1884
McCormick dies

Inventor of Coca-Cola

John Pemberton

1831–1888

When you think of a soft drink, there are many that come to mind, but probably near the top of the list is Coca-Cola. This drink entered the world in the nineteenth century and has influenced cultures and societies around the world ever since. Today it is known widely as Coke, and this name is even used in some areas to define every soft drink brand. Its significance as a beverage cannot be ignored. When John Pemberton, a Georgia chemist and doctor, invented this revolutionary drink, little did he suspect how popular it would become.

Beginnings

Pemberton lived his entire life in Georgia—from his birth, on January 8, 1831, in Knoxville, through his childhood in Rome, to his college days in Macon and his later years as a chemist, doctor, and businessman in Columbus and Atlanta. He studied medicine and pharmacy at the Reform Medical College of Georgia, where at age nineteen he earned a license to practice Thomsonian medicine, a type of medicine based on herbal remedies and elixirs that was popular in the nineteenth century.

John Pemberton, creator of Coca-Cola

Defining the Problem

In 1855, Pemberton founded J.S. Pemberton and Company of Columbus, a very successful business selling the basic chemical elements in elixirs. After serving in the Third Georgia Cavalry Battalion during the Civil War, Pemberton returned to his life in medicine. In 1869, he moved his laboratories to Atlanta. They were an impressive operation. A reporter from the *Atlanta Constitution* called them "one of the most splendid chemical laboratories that there is in the country."

Pemberton himself relocated to Atlanta shortly after establishing his labs and soon became a trustee of the Atlanta Medical College; in 1881, he joined the first state examining board for pharmacists in Georgia. Indeed, he was one of the more highly regarded men in medicine in Atlanta. He also developed many popular elixirs, including Extract of Styllinger, Globe of Flower Cough Syrup, Indian Queen Hair Dye, Triplex Liver Pills, and the **progenitor** of Coca-Cola: Pemberton's French Wine Coca.

Inventors of Food and Agriculture Technology

Designing the Solution

French Wine Coca was a nerve tonic, stimulant, and headache remedy, and nearly every druggist in Atlanta sold it. The tonic was made primarily of wine, the extracts of Peruvian coca leaves, and West African kola nuts.

Pemberton had based his elixir on a popular European type of coca wine, Vin Mariani, that had been developed in Paris in 1863. Like Vin Mariani, Pemberton's French Wine Coca relied on the medicinal qualities of the coca plant, which for more than two thousand years had been used by the indigenous peoples of Peru and Bolivia as a stimulant, digestive aid, aphrodisiac, and purported life extender. Pemberton improved on Vin Mariani by adding, among other things, extracts of the kola nut, a stimulant rich in caffeine. In 1885, Pemberton described his elixir to a reporter from the *Atlanta Journal* as "the most excellent of all tonics, assisting digestion, imparting energy to the organs of respiration, and strengthening the muscular and nervous systems."

In 1886, Atlanta fell to the growing temperance movement, which sought to outlaw the consumption of liquor, and the city enacted a law prohibiting the sale of alcoholic beverages. Despite the popularity of his wine-based tonic, Pemberton knew he would have to stop selling it. He channeled his efforts into developing an alcohol-free version that would still retain the medicinal benefits of the coca leaves and kola nuts.

Pemberton worked tirelessly on his new formula. During this time, his nephew described him as an obsessed and even secretive inventor, working into the night and often missing meals. Finally, by replacing wine with sugar syrup, citric acid, and various oils, Pemberton developed what came to be known as Coca-Cola. Legend has it that the original was made in a three-legged brass kettle in his backyard and that Pemberton himself walked the jug of syrup to the pharmacy where it was first sold.

Applying the Solution

Although Pemberton developed the recipe, Coca-Cola the brand was created by Pemberton's bookkeeper, Frank Robinson.

Robinson developed the alliterative name Coca-Cola and changed the *k* of the kola nut to a *c*, for added visual effect. He also drew the unmistakable pair of scripted *C*'s that still defines the brand today.

The first Coca-Cola was sold by Willis Venable, the self-styled "Soda Water King of the South," at the soda fountain in Jacob's Pharmacy in Atlanta on May 8, 1886. It cost five cents. In Coca-Cola Company lore, customers immediately declared the drink "excellent," and "delicious and refreshing." Another piece of Coca-Cola lore suggests that Venable "accidentally" put carbonated water into Pemberton's syrup—a story that has persisted despite being false. In truth, the numbers suggest that the initial response was lukewarm. Just 25 gallons (95 liters) of Coca-Cola syrup were sold that first year: about nine servings total per day and less than $50 (around $1,280 US in 2014) in sales. Production costs for that same period totaled more than $70 (around $1,790 US in 2014).

Pemberton nevertheless continued to push Coca-Cola as "the Great National Temperance Drink," and the company blanketed Atlanta with free drink coupons. Business picked up. In March 1888, Pemberton filed incorporation papers for the Coca-Cola Company in the Fulton County Superior Court, even though, in the wake of the repeal of Atlanta's prohibition laws in 1887, his true interest lay in reviving his French Wine Coca. He left his son, Charles, to look after the production of Coca-Cola, and he eventually sold his interests in the business to other investors. Pemberton sold his final shares to Asa G. Candler, a fellow Georgia businessman, who by 1891 had acquired control of the entire company for just $2,300 (around $60,700 US in 2014). Five months after founding the Coca-Cola Company, Pemberton died. His son died a few years later, leaving the company in the hands of other investors.

Pemberton's Legacy Continues

Asa Candler transformed Pemberton's temperance drink into one of the most successful and recognizable national and global brands. Candler emphasized advertising early on, to great success. By 1892, he had increased sales of Coca-Cola syrup tenfold. Under Candler, Coca-Cola went from a fountain drink to a bottled drink. Candler also began the great tradition of Coca-Cola branded products, from glasses to calendars, clocks, and even urns—many of which have become collectible items.

Under Candler, Coca-Cola's advertising was relentlessly upbeat, as it remains today. Indeed, Coca-Cola's association with happiness

Coca-Cola's Influence on Santa

Prior to the 1930s, Santa Claus was depicted around the world in many different ways. Sometimes he was a tall, gaunt man dressed in green. Other times he was a scary-looking elf. Coca-Cola changed the perception of Santa Claus starting in 1931, when it created magazine ad campaigns featuring Santa Claus. The company hired Michigan-born cartoonist Haddon Sundblom to draw him. Sundblom hired his friend, Lou Prentiss, a retired salesman, as a model for his assignment. The resulting image became a well-known character for Coca-Cola's ads: a portly old man in a bright red suit. Coca-Cola liked this depiction of Santa and used this concept in all of its holiday advertisements for decades after. As years passed and

marketing campaigns continued, many people began to think of Santa Claus as a jolly old man dressed in a suit of red. He would often be shown delivering toys and sometimes playing with them or enjoying an ice cold Coke. It was in this way that Coca-Cola could be considered responsible for creating the modern-day Santa Claus.

Coca-Cola advertisements changed the way people thought of and pictured Santa Claus.

belied some of the more unseemly aspects of the product in the early part of the twentieth century. In 1903, a scandal arose over presence of cocaine in the drink, albeit in small amounts. Although Candler changed the recipe to remove the cocaine, adding citric acid and flavored oils in its place, the drink continued to have a negative reputation with the Federal Bureau of Chemistry, which, in 1907, sent an agent to Atlanta to investigate the effects of drinking Coca-Cola. The report described "Coca-Cola fiends" roaming the streets and expressed deep concern because children as young as four were allowed to consume the beverage. Headlines from the time screamed, "Eight Coca-Colas Contain Enough Caffeine to Kill."

Nevertheless, Coca-Cola survived and prospered. Under the company's next president, Robert Woodruff, Coca-Cola was marketed around the globe. With troops stationed abroad during World War II, Coca-Cola was introduced to Europe and beyond. "We'll see that every man in uniform gets a bottle of Coca-Cola for five cents," Woodruff declared, "wherever he is and whatever it costs our company." New trends in the beverage industry, such as the six-pack, and contracts with burgeoning fast-food chains and movie theaters in the 1950s and 1960s brought Coca-Cola to nearly every corner of the United States. In the 1960s and 1970s, Coca-Cola began to expand its product line, introducing brands such as Fanta, Sprite, Tab, and Fresca.

In 1982, when Roberto Goizueta was its president, Coca-Cola replaced the original formula with New Coke, a slightly sweeter and less carbonated version of Coca-Cola, which had tested well in focus groups. Critics declared that New Coke was one of the worst marketing disasters in business history. Wrote one customer, "Changing Coke is like God making the grass purple." Within seventy-eight days, Coca-Cola announced the return of the original recipe. However, the failure of New Coke only proved what a spectacular success Coca-Cola—the brand perhaps more than the drink itself—had become over the previous century.

The Impact of the Solution on Society

Although Coca-Cola's success was the result of many people, its creator, John Pemberton, lives on in the drink's history as an innovative and ambitious individual. Without him, Coca-Cola would not exist today. It was his secret recipe and his business tactics that led the drink and its company to become the sensations they have evolved into today.

Coca-Cola has had a profound effect on the world. It is an instantly recognizable brand and has even changed the image of Santa Claus. Coca-Cola is found in every corner of the globe, and it continues to be a top seller in soft drink consumption. However, there is concern that frequent consumption of Coke can affect someone's health by leading to problems such as obesity or diabetes. Many people are trying to dissuade others from drinking the beverage too often. Nevertheless, the company and its drink will remain popular for years to come.

Timeline

1831
John Smith Pemberton born in Knoxville, Georgia

1850
Pemberton earns his medical license

1855
Pemberton founds J.S. Pemberton and Company of Columbus

1886
The first Coca-Cola is sold in Atlanta

1888
Pemberton files incorporation papers for the Coca-Cola Company and dies later that year

Clarence Saunders

1881–1953

Over the years, there have been many changes in the food industry. One of the most significant advancements in the twentieth century was the introduction of self-service grocery stores. The man responsible for this invention was Clarence Saunders, a businessman from Tennessee. He envisioned a store where people shopped for their groceries themselves. Eventually he made this vision into a reality, and the modern grocery store was born.

Growing Up

Clarence Saunders was born in Virginia in 1881, but his family relocated to Tennessee when he was still young. His family was not wealthy, and at age fourteen, he left school to clerk in a general store.

By his twenties, Saunders was working for a wholesale grocer in Memphis, selling products directly to various grocers. Later he became a citywide salesman for another wholesaler.

Clarence Saunders

Defining the Problem

His experiences with grocers taught him that credit losses, high overhead, and inefficiency—common features of the early-twentieth-century grocery store—often doomed a small business to failure.

Designing the Solution

On September 16, 1916, Saunders opened his own grocery store, called Piggly Wiggly. There are various stories about the origins of the name, but Saunders's standard answer to the question, "Why did you name it Piggly Wiggly?" was, "So people will ask that very question!" Located at 79 Jefferson Street in downtown Memphis, it was unlike any store of its time.

Typically, people shopped for groceries and other goods in a market or general store. Shoppers would enter the store and ask the clerk for the goods they wanted. The clerk stood behind a counter, along with the store's entire inventory. He would pull items from the shelves; measure out quantities from the jars, boxes, or barrels; then tally the costs and add the total to a customer's account. This process translated into lengthy interactions, high labor costs, and, in general, higher prices for customers.

Piggly Wiggly was different. It had shopping baskets, open shelves, checkout stands, and turnstiles (an invention patented by Saunders) at every entrance. Customers would walk along the aisles and select groceries themselves, without the aid of a clerk. Each item was marked with its price.

Saunders added other features that changed the shopping experience, including a uniformed staff, elaborate aisle displays, and many nationally advertised products. He instituted one-way aisles to smooth the flow of traffic and to force customers to view all the products. By cutting down on labor costs, he was able to sell goods more cheaply. He further appealed to cost-conscious shoppers with his cash-only policy. At other groceries, the charges were added to customers' accounts, but at Piggly Wiggly all customers paid in cash at the time of purchase. One advertisement read, "Your dollar at Piggly Wiggly will not help pay the BAD DEBTS of others."

Saunders submitted a six-page patent application for his innovations, and in 1917 he received a patent for the "self-serving store," which he described as "distributing the merchandise of a store in such a manner that goods may be selected and taken by the customers themselves while making a circuitous path through the store."

Applying the Solution

Though many doubted Saunders at first, Piggly Wiggly quickly became a roaring success. Soon, new franchises opened up around the country, particularly in the South and Southeast. Each was identical—the same design and patented fixtures were used in every store. Saunders advertised his chain heavily, and the Piggly Wiggly name and logo grew to be not just recognizable but beloved. By 1922, Piggly Wiggly Corporation was the second-largest grocery chain in the United States, with 1,200 stores in 29 states. The chain dominated the market in Kansas City, Missouri, and San Antonio, Texas. A decade later, Piggly Wiggly Corporation, now 2,600 stores strong, made more then $180 million per year.

Piggly Wiggly earned Saunders incredible wealth, and he was not afraid to display it. A well-known eccentric, Saunders commissioned a 38,000-square-foot (3,530 sq m) mansion in Memphis to be built from pink marble. It was to feature an indoor pool and a shooting range. A dispute with stockbrokers in New York, however, brought an end to Saunders's reign at Piggly Wiggly, and Saunders never slept a night in his dream mansion.

In 1932, stockbrokers tried to bring down the price of Piggly Wiggly stock, which had been on the market for some time. Incensed, Saunders allegedly took a train to New York with a suitcase full of cash, hoping to buy back the stock in his own company. In the end, Saunders was forced to declare bankruptcy and give up control of Piggly Wiggly Corporation. His ornate marble house was donated to the city and turned into the Pink Palace Museum.

Saunders went on to create other grocery store chains, with an eye toward automation. The next chain was called, oddly enough, "Clarence Saunders, Sole Owner of My Name Stores." (Saunders was reacting, it is believed, to his having to give up all rights to the name he had coined, "Piggly Wiggly.") Although reasonably successful, the chain was forced to close during the Great Depression. Then, in 1937, Saunders founded another Memphis grocery, Keydoozle.

With Keydoozle, a play on "Key Does All," Saunders took the idea of self-service to another level. Keydoozle was one of the first mechanical, automated grocery stores—not unlike a very large vending machine. All the merchandise in the store was displayed in a series of glass cabinets. The customer indicated how many of each item she or he wanted by pushing a special key into a keyhole and

The Great Supermarket Debate

Clarence Saunders is acknowledged as the inventor of the self-service grocery, but surprisingly, he is not the man behind the supermarket. For many years, there was debate about the true founder of the supermarket. Then, in 1980, the Food Marketing Institute, in conjunction with the Smithsonian Institution and with funding from the H.J. Heinz Corporation (of Heinz ketchup fame), set out to settle the question. According to the Smithsonian's researchers, the first supermarket was invented by Michael Cullen, who opened a King Kullen store in Jamaica, Queens, New York, in 1930. Although Saunders had brought the world self-service, uniform stores, and nationwide marketing, Cullen was the one who built on that idea by adding separate food departments, selling large volumes of food at discount prices, and adding a parking lot.

Today, self-service checkout systems are in place in many grocery stores around the world.

pulling the trigger to indicate quantity. This information was recorded on a paper tape. Machinery in the back of the store was used to assemble the order and to send the products, via conveyor belt, to the checkout stand. The tape was used to tally the bill, and the groceries were boxed and ready to go. Keydoozle used space and human labor more efficiently, but the machinery—much of which Saunders built himself—was faulty and the store ultimately failed.

Undaunted even as he neared his one-hundredth birthday, Saunders began drawing up plans for yet another store, the Foodelectric. This store held the promise of full automation. In a 1950s business book, *TNT: The Power Within You*, Saunders described his plans for Foodelectric to the author: "The store operates so automatically that the customer can collect her groceries herself, wrap them and act as her own cashier. It eliminates the checkout crush, cuts overhead expenses and enables a small staff to handle a tremendous volume … I can handle a $2 million volume with only eight employees." However, the store, which was to be located two blocks from the first Piggly Wiggly store in downtown Memphis, never opened. Clarence Saunders died in October 1953.

The Impact of the Solution on Society

Saunders's vision of automation was clearly ahead of its time, as was his interest in and enthusiasm for self-service. Indeed, the first Piggly

Inventors of Food and Agriculture Technology

Wiggly predated other stores of its kind by at least two decades. At the time Saunders was dreaming of the Foodelectric, the supermarket, carrying all the hallmarks of Piggly Wiggly grocery stores, had just started to become a regular part of American life.

Saunders did not live to see the rise of the self-service economy—from the birth of laundromats, cafeterias, and self-service car washes to more recent high-tech examples, such as online shopping or airport kiosks that allow self-service check-in—although he may have been one of the first individuals to realize its potential. Nevertheless, today many of Saunders's inventions have become a reality. Modern grocery stores and supermarkets incorporate his layout and cashier ideas, and more and more often, automatic checkout lanes, equipped with scanners, credit card machines, and computer systems that engage the customer, are available in the store. It is without a doubt that Clarence Saunders changed the grocery industry forever and created a revolutionary concept that still flourishes today.

Timeline

1881
Clarence Saunders born in Virginia; his family soon relocates to Tennessee

1916
Saunders opens the first Piggly Wiggly store

1917
Saunders patents his self-service store plan

1922
Piggly Wiggly is the second-largest grocery chain in the United States

1932
Saunders is forced to declare bankruptcy

1937
Saunders founds the Keydoozle store

1953
Saunders dies

Inventor of the Cotton Gin

Eli Whitney

1765–1825

There are many inventions that have improved life for many people around the world, but few inventions have rivaled the significance of the cotton gin. Prior to its creation, cotton was picked and the seeds separated by hand. It was a painstaking process that took many long hours to complete. Usually the people doing this were living in the South, where weather conditions were often very hot and humid. The cotton gin made it possible for farmers to separate cotton's parts better and more quickly. This benefited life for southern workers and farmers, and it later led to an influx of slaves on southern plantations. Eli Whitney, the man responsible for inventing this revolutionary device, is recognized today as a well-known inventor whose ideas moved society into a more modern time.

The Road to Invention

Eli Whitney was born on December 8, 1765, in Westborough, Massachusetts. Although he was the son of a farmer, he preferred tinkering in the workshop to working in the fields, and his great mechanical skill soon became obvious. At the age of eight, he repaired his father's watch; by the age of twelve, he was building and repairing violins. Within a few years, he invented a machine for making nails and set himself up in business.

The good-natured teenager was 6 feet (1.8 m) tall, was broad-shouldered, and had large hands—perfect for farm work. Whitney, however, longed to go to college, but his family was poor and he had to earn the money for his studies. Between the ages of eighteen and twenty-four, he worked as an elementary school teacher, earning $7 a month. In 1779, using the money he had saved and with help from his father, he entered Yale College (now Yale University) to study law. To earn money, he continued his nail-making business, made hat pins, and even repaired a valuable **orrery** belonging to the college president.

Graduating from Yale at age twenty-six, he was penniless and unsure what the future held. He was offered a teaching job in South Carolina, but the employer changed his mind and refused to pay Whitney as much as they had agreed. When another job came up in Georgia, Whitney made the long journey south—only to find that this offer had fallen through as well. Then he met Catherine Littlefield Greene (1753–1814), the wealthy widow of General Nathanael Greene, a hero of the American Revolution. She took pity on Whitney and invited him to stay at her home, Mulberry Grove, a cotton plantation near Savannah, Georgia.

Defining the Problem

One evening in 1793, Catherine Greene and her guests were discussing the cotton business. England's demand for cotton was great because of the invention of spinning and weaving machines, but cotton growers in southern states like Georgia could not satisfy the need. The problem was that green-seed (or short-staple) cotton was difficult to process because the cotton fibers, the part of the plant used to make cloth, stuck to the seeds. Separating the seeds from the fibers by hand took a long time, making the product uneconomical. A different kind of cotton called black-seed (or long-staple) was easier to process because the seeds and fibers did not stick together. Black-seed cotton, however, was hard to grow inland; it grew well only near the coast.

As Catherine Greene and her guests discussed this problem, she challenged Whitney, who had impressed her with his skills by fixing things around her home, to build a machine that would clean green-seed cotton. Perhaps it was just a joke among friends around the dinner table, but Whitney took up the challenge.

Designing the Solution

Although Whitney had never seen cotton plants, he soon figured out how to solve the problem: he needed to make a comb that could pull the cotton fibers away from their seeds. Within ten days, he had built a working model of a cotton-combing machine. Catherine Greene and her young plantation manager, Phineas Miller, were impressed—Miller so much so that he offered to go into business with Whitney to manufacture the machine.

Whitney had studied law, so he knew about the new Patent Act of 1793. This allowed inventors to use a patent to protect "any useful art, manufacture, engine, machine, or device, or any instrument thereon not before known or used." A patent was a drawing with a written description of an invention that went on public record. Taking out a patent gave inventors fourteen years to make money from their ideas before the ideas became freely available for others to copy.

By 1794, Whitney and Miller acquired their patent and put the cotton gin into production at a factory in New Haven, Connecticut. Obstacles arose almost immediately. If Whitney had manufactured his machine the traditional way, each worker would have made an entire gin, but he wanted each worker to assemble only one small part of the gin before passing the machine on to another worker to make the next part. This early version of the modern assembly line was quicker for Whitney, but much less interesting for the workers. Many were craftsmen who resented this way of working, and some quit. Epidemics of scarlet fever and yellow fever then struck

An illustration of Eli Whitney

New Haven, claiming 114 lives and reducing Whitney's workforce. On March 11, 1795, fire broke out in Whitney's factory and destroyed almost the entire building.

Applying the Solution

By now, plantation owners had started growing green-seed cotton, and the demand for Whitney's new machine increased daily. With their factory plagued with problems, Whitney and Miller could not make all the cotton gins they had promised. They had agreed not to sell their machine but to rent it to the growers for a 30 to 40 percent cut of their cotton profits. They did not realize just how much green-seed cotton would be grown and that they could have settled for a much smaller cut and still become immensely rich. Also, the growers thought they were greedy and refused to pay so much. They realized how simple Whitney's machine was and started making their own.

An Unlikely Invention

A few pieces of wood and metal fastened together—it is hard to imagine that such a thing could make fortunes, help spark a civil war, and change the history of a nation. These simple components of Eli Whitney's cotton gin, a machine that could split cotton plants into their useful parts, did all this.

Cotton plants grow to roughly 1 foot (0.3 m) high in about two months, when white blooms form. When the flowers fall off, they leave behind a small green pod called a boll. The boll continues to grow and after another six to eight weeks is roughly the size and shape of an egg. Inside are several compartments, each containing perhaps ten seeds and each seed sprouting thousands of fluffy cotton fibers. Most of the world's cotton is the green-seed (short-staple) variety, in which the seeds and the fibers stick closely together. To make useful cotton for textiles, the seeds and the fibers must be separated.

Before Eli Whitney invented the cotton gin, this job was done by hand, with an entire day needed to separate the seeds from just

Whitney tried to stop them from violating his patent, but a loophole in the patent law left him powerless. Too late, Whitney and Miller drastically cut the price of their gin. By 1797, the two enterprising partners were deep in debt and they went out of business.

In 1798, green-seed cotton was growing throughout the South and the growers were getting rich. Whitney had made all this possible, yet he was penniless and his patent seemed useless. When the patent law changed in 1800, the partners were able to take new legal action. As a result, after 1802, the states of South Carolina, North Carolina, Tennessee and, finally, Georgia were forced to pay to use the cotton gin. Whitney and Miller fought sixty separate suits by 1807 and earned around $90,000—a huge sum in those days—but the money was eaten up by debts and legal costs. When Whitney's fourteen-year patent on the cotton gin expired in 1807, there was more bad news: Congress refused to renew it. Whitney commented bitterly, "An invention can be so valuable as to be worthless to the inventor." He would never patent anything again.

1 pound (0.5 kg) of cotton fiber. Using Whitney's gin, a cotton worker could clean the seeds from the fibers by stuffing raw cotton into one end of the machine and turning a handle. Whitney's machine made a dramatic improvement: in a single day, it could clean fifty times as much cotton as fifty people working by hand. Whitney wrote to his father: "Tis generally said by those who know anything about it that I shall make a fortune by it."

Others copied Whitney's invention and cotton gins started to vary in design, but they all worked in broadly the same way with a comb and hooks on a rotating cylinder, just as Whitney had designed them. Small gins were hand-cranked; larger ones, driven by mules or water wheels, were soon in operation; steam-powered gins followed soon after. Although today's gins are huge, factory-sized machines powered by electricity, they still work on a principle similar to the one Whitney discovered.

By now, Whitney had a new business. In the late 1790s, he had decided to seek a different way of making money. First, he proposed printing stamps for the US government. When that idea fell through, he thought of making muskets. Many muskets were imported from Europe, but as America neared war with France in the 1790s, the US government realized that it needed to manufacture its own weapons. Although an enormous **armory** had been set up in Springfield, Massachusetts, in 1794, making guns was a slow process; each weapon was made laboriously by one worker. Whitney thought he could speed production using the methods from his cotton gin factory. In a bold and risky move, he persuaded the government to sign a contract with him to supply ten thousand muskets for $134,000 in just twenty-eight months. At this point, he had no factory, had no workers, and had yet to produce a musket.

Two years later, Whitney had still not produced so much as a single musket. It took him more than ten years to complete the contract. During that time, he revolutionized the way guns were made. At the armory he built in Hamden, Connecticut, 2 miles (3.2 km) outside New Haven, he introduced a production-line system in which many unskilled workers each made part of a musket before passing it on to the next person. Instead of being individually handcrafted, all the guns were made to a standard design so the parts from one gun could fit any other. Whitney was one of the first to manufacture goods with interchangeable parts. Instead of using human or animal power, he sited his factory near the Mill River and used water power to operate his machines. Learning from his experience with unhappy cotton gin workers, he turned his factory into a friendly community called Whitneyville. Apart from providing housing and food for the musket makers, he offered education and training to their children.

Whitney became rich making muskets, not as the inventor of the cotton gin as he had hoped. Even so, much of his life seemed to have passed him by: he was already in his twenties when he became a student, legal battles over the cotton gin exhausted him during his thirties, and his forties were spent getting his arms factory off the ground.

In letters he wrote to his old friend Catherine Greene, he spoke of being a "solitary old bachelor." However, not for long. He married Henrietta Edwards, the granddaughter of famous preacher Jonathan Edwards, in 1817. His two nephews, Philos and Eli Whitney Blake, took over running his factory in 1820, and the same year Whitney and Henrietta had a son. By now, Whitney was in his mid-fifties and in poor health. He died five years later, on January 8, 1825.

Eli Whitney's invention made cotton collection and production easier.

The Impact of the Solution on Society

During the nineteenth century, Whitney's cotton gin changed the face of agriculture in the United States because it made green-seed cotton economical and increased enormously the amount of cotton planted and harvested. By 1800, in the five or six years after the cotton gin was invented, cotton production had increased twenty-five-fold and in every decade thereafter production doubled. In 1850, the

United States was growing around three-quarters of all the world's cotton. This cotton brought huge prosperity to the southern states east of the Mississippi River, which grew around 60 percent of the nation's entire crop. Seeing the staggering profits to be made, farmers switched from other crops such as rice and tobacco. The "cotton belt" (the cotton-growing area of the United States) also expanded greatly. Today, it stretches across the South from coast to coast (although little cotton is grown in the states of Florida, Nevada, and Virginia).

Whitney's cotton gin also had a dramatic effect on the history of the United States by breathing new life into the slave trade. When Whitney invented his machine in 1793, slavery was almost a thing of the past. Plantation owners were using slaves in only six states, and even though slave labor was cheap, it was still one of their biggest costs. Many owners either had released their slaves or planned to do so; the slave trade seemed to be gradually dying out. Then Whitney's cotton gin appeared, making growing cotton immensely profitable throughout the South. The gin did away with the need for some human labor because it automated cotton cleaning, but more people were needed to pick cotton from the fields. In the twenty years following the invention of the gin, eighty thousand slaves were imported from Africa to work on the southern plantations. Congress banned the importing of slaves in 1808, but slavery continued to flourish. By 1860, the number of states using slave labor had grown from six to fifteen, and around one-third of all the people in the South (nearly four million people) were slaves.

Although the Civil War had many causes, slavery was one of the most important: people in the North believed slavery should be abolished because they saw it as cruel, immoral, and inhuman; those in the South wanted to preserve slavery because they saw it as essential to the South's prosperity and as part of the region's culture. A crisis was reached in 1860 after the election of Abraham Lincoln to the presidency on an antislavery ticket. The Civil War between the North and the South began the following year. Around 260,000 Southerners were killed, many by mass-produced muskets made at the Whitney armory in New Haven. Whitney's cotton gin had brought prosperity to the South; now his rifles brought the region defeat.

Eli Whitney is known today for his contribution to agriculture as well as for the assembly line method utilized in his factories. Today the cotton gin remains a part of the agricultural industry, and his assembly line concept became remarkably successful once Henry Ford adopted it for his company in the early twentieth century. This process is still used in companies today. There is no doubt that Eli Whitney was a man with many ideas, all of which came to be but varied in degrees of success. Still, he is considered an important contributor to modern inventions, and his name will live on history.

Timeline

1765
Eli Whitney born in
Westborough, Massachusetts

1779
Whitney enters Yale College

1791
Whitney graduates from Yale

1793
Whitney develops a working
model of the cotton gin

1794
Whitney begins manufacturing
cotton gins

1795
A fire destroys most of Whitney's
cotton gin factory

1797
Whitney goes into debt and out
of business

1807
Whitney pioneers the
technique of mass production,
manufacturing muskets for
the US government; Whitney's
patent expires

1825
Whitney dies

Glossary

additive A product added to another product to keep it fresh.

aerate To dig up land and by doing so increase the amount of air in between soil particles.

agriculture Cultivating land to make food and other products.

armory An arms-making plant.

biopharming Using principles of genetic engineering to insert genetic material useful for pharmaceuticals into crops that would not otherwise have that material. This results in genetically modified crops.

biotechnology Using human ingenuity to harness natural, biological processes.

botany The study of plants.

canola Oilseed rape grown to create cooking oil. It was developed in Canada and is grown in North America.

cotton boll The growing head of a cotton plant.

cradle A scythe with a wooden frame attached.

cross-pollination The transfer of pollen from one plant to another plant.

DNA Deoxyribonucleic acid; the basic genetic instructions that tell cells how to grow.

domesticate To tame.

genetically modified organism (GMO) An organism, such as a plant, that is injected with genetic material from another organism.

green Good for the environment.

horticulturalist A person who collects and breeds plants.

hunter-gatherer A person who hunts animals and collects berries, nuts, and other edible food from the earth.

hybridization The act of taking related species of plants or animals and breeding them to make a new plant or animal.

mercerize To give cotton its luster or shine.

nap The fuzzy surface of a carpet.

nodule A plant bud.

orrery A complicated clockwork model of the planets.

pathology The study of diseases.

progenitor An original concept that serves as a guide or pattern for future improvements.

scythe A curved blade meant for cutting shrubs, tall grasses, and brush.

spiritualism Belief in the ability to contact the dead through a medium, or a person who can go in between the states of the living and the dead.

taxidermy The practice of preserving animals after they have died.

testimonial A quotation from a satisfied customer that praises a product.

thresher A machine that separates the useful part of a crop, such as the grain, from the unwanted part, which is known as chaff.

transgenic An adjective used to describe an organism, such as a plant, that contains genetic material artificially introduced from another organism.

tuber A root/stem formed underground.

Underground Railroad The system of paths and homes that helped escaped slaves from the South find refuge in the North.

Further Information

Introduction to Food and Agriculture Technology

Books   Mazoyer, Marcel, and Laurence Roudart. *A History of World Agriculture: From the Neolithic Age to the Current Crisis.* New York: Monthly Review Press, 2006.

Toussaint-Samant, Maguelonne. *A History of Food.* Oxford, England: Wiley-Blackwell, 2008.

Websites   **Crash Course: The Agricultural Revolution**
www.youtube.com/watch?v=Yocja_N5s1l

Growing Nation: The History of Agriculture in America
www.agclassroom.org/gan/timeline

Nicolas-François Appert: Pioneer in Food Preservation

Book   Kelly, Ian. *Cooking for Kings.* New York: Walker & Company, 2005.

Websites   **Encyclopedia Britannica: Nicolas-François Appert**
www.britannica.com/EBchecked/topic/30573/Nicolas-Appert

Stuff of Genius: Nicolas Appert and Canned Goods
shows.howstuffworks.com/stuff-of-genius/41738-napoleon-and-canned-food-the-story-of-nicolas-appert-video.htm

Clarence Birdseye: Inventor of the Frozen Food Industry

Books   Alexander, Paul. *Frozen: How American Ingenuity Created the TV Dinner and Changed the Way We Eat.* Seattle, WA: Thirteen Publishing Company, 2013.

Kurlansky, Mark. *Frozen in Time: Clarence Birdseye's Outrageous Idea About Frozen Food.* New York: Random House Children's Books, 2014.

Websites   **Birds Eye Foods**
www.birdseye.com/vegetable-products/explore-by-product

Who Made America?: Clarence Birdseye Biography
www.pbs.org/wgbh/theymadeamerica/whomade/birdseye_hi.html

Norman Borlaug: Developer of Improved Wheat

Books   Barber, Dan. *The Third Plate: Field Notes on the Future of Food*. New York: Penguin Press, 2014.

               Hesser, Leon. *The Man Who Fed the World*. New York: Park East Press, 2010.

Websites   **Norman Borlaug and the Green Revolution**
www.youtube.com/watch?v=Lg9-HTtgFOk

               Norman Borlaug Heritage Foundation
www.normanborlaug.org

Jacques Brandenberger: Inventor of Cellophane

Books   Chetwynd, Josh. *How the Hot Dog Found Its Bun: Accidental Discoveries and Unexplained Inspirations That Shape What We Eat and Drink*. Guildford, CT: Globe Pequot Press, 2012.

               Krols, Birgit. *Accidental Inventions: The Chance Discoveries That Changed Our Lives*. San Rafael, CA: Insight Editions, 2012.

Websites   **Encyclopedia Britannica: Cellophane**
www.britannica.com/EBchecked/101586/cellophane

               Stuff of Genius: Jacques Brandenberger and Cellophane
www.geniusstuff.com/video/clips/40377-the-stuff-of-genius-cellophane-video

Edwin Beard Budding: Inventor of the Reel Lawn Mower

Books   Bryson, Bill. *At Home: A Short History of Private Life*. New York: Penguin, 2010.

               Lloyd, John, John Mitchinson, and James Harkin. *1,227 Quite Interesting Facts to Blow Your Socks Off*. New York: W.W. Norton, 2013.

Websites   **A History of the Lawn Mower**
www.bbc.co.uk/ahistoryoftheworld/objects/NI2ZjBwpTcqYdtpXFnIzUQ

Further Information

Who Made the Lawn Mower?
www.nytimes.com/2012/03/18/magazine/who-made-that-lawn-mower.html

Luther Burbank: Inventor of New Plant Varieties

Book Smith, Jane S. *The Garden of Invention: Luther Burbank and the Business of Breeding Plants*. New York: Penguin, 2009.

Websites **Biography of Luther Burbank**
www.britannica.com/EBchecked/topic/84930/Luther-Burbank

Luther Burbank Home and Gardens
www.lutherburbank.org

George Washington Carver: Developer of Industrial Uses for Agricultural Products

Books Clark, Glenn. *The Man Who Talks with the Flowers: An Intimate Life Story of Dr. George Washington Carver*. African American Heritage series. Seattle, WA: Wilder Publications, 2011.

Kremer, Gary R. *George Washington Carver: A Biography*. Santa Barbara, CA: Greenwood, 2011.

Websites **Biography of George Washington Carver**
www.biography.com/people/george-washington-carver-9240299

George Washington Carver
www.history.com/topics/black-history/george-washington-carver

John Deere: Inventor of the Improved, Steel Plow

Book Dahlstrom, Neil, and Jeremy Dahlstrom. *The John Deere Story: A Biography of Plowmakers John and Charles Deere*. De Kalb, IL: Northern Illinois University Press, 2005.

Websites **Biography of John Deere**
www.biography.com/people/john-deere-9269591

John Deere Worldwide
www.deere.com/en_US/regional_home.page

Robert T. Fraley, Mary-Dell Chilton, and Marc Van Montagu: Inventors of Genetically Modified Crops

Books   Ferry, Natalie, and Angharad M. R. Gatehouse, eds. *Environmental Impact of Genetically Modified Crops*. Wallingford, Oxfordshire, England: CABI, 2009.

Hillstrom, Kevin. *Genetically Modified Foods*. Health and Nutrition. Independence, KY: Lucent Books, 2012.

Websites   **How Are GMOs Created?**
www.youtube.com/watch?v=2G-yUuiqIZ0

The World Food Prize: 2013 Laureates
www.worldfoodprize.org/index.
cfm?nodeID=66969&audienceID=1

Lloyd A. Hall: Inventor of Food Preservation Methods

Book   Jango-Cohen, Judith. *The History of Food*. Major Inventions Through History. Minneapolis, MN: Lerner Classroom, 2006.

Website   **Biography of Lloyd Augustus Hall**
www.encyclopedia.com/doc/1G2-2506300079.html

Amanda Jones: Inventor of Vacuum Canning

Books   Coppens, Linda Miles. *What American Women Did, 1789–1920*. Jefferson, NC: McFarland, 2007.

Vare, Ethlie Ann, and Greg Ptacek. *Patently Female: From AZT to TV Dinners, Stories of Women Inventors and Their Breakthrough Ideas*. New York: John Wiley & Sons, 2002.

Websites   **Biography of Amanda Jones**
inventors.about.com/library/inventors/bljones.htm

Definition of Spiritualism
www.britannica.com/EBchecked/topic/560501/spiritualism

Will Keith Kellogg: Inventor of Corn Flakes

Books   Gitlin, Marty, and Topher Ellis. *The Great American Cereal Books: How Breakfast Got Its Crunch*. New York: Abrams, 2012.

Further Information

Mattern, Joanne. *The Kellogg Family: Breakfast Cereal Pioneers*. Edina, MN: Checkerboard Books, 2011.

Websites **Cornflake Kings: The Kellogg Brothers**
www.youtube.com/watch?v=Pgygluf8b8E

Official Website of Kellogg's Cereal
www.kelloggs.com/en_US/home.html

Cyrus Hall McCormick: Inventor of the Mechanical Reaper

Books Green, James. *Death in the Haymarket: A Story of Chicago, the First Labor Movement, and the Bombing That Divided Gilded Age America*. New York: Anchor Books, 2007.

Masur, Louis P. *1831: Year of Eclipse*. New York: Hill and Wang, 2001.

Websites **Entry on Reaper**
www.britannica.com/EBchecked/topic/493183/reaper

People and Events: Cyrus McCormick
www.pbs.org/wgbh/amex/chicago/peopleevents/p_mccormick.html

John Pemberton: Inventor of Coca-Cola

Books Isdell, Neville, and David Beasley. *Inside Coca-Cola: A CEO's Life Story of Building the World's Most Popular Brand*. New York: St. Martin's Press, 2011.

Pendergast, Mark. *For God, Country and Coca-Cola: The Definitive History of the Great American Soft Drink and the Company That Makes It*. 3rd ed. New York: Basic Books, 2013.

Websites **History of Coca-Cola**
www.coca-colacompany.com/topics/heritage

Official Website of Coca-Cola
us.coca-cola.com

Clarence Saunders: Inventor of the Self-Service Grocery Store

Book Freeman, Mike. *Clarence Saunders and the Founding of Piggly Wiggly: The Rise & Fall of a Memphis Maverick*. Charleston, SC: The History Press, 2011.

Website   **Piggly Wiggly: About Us**
www.pigglywiggly.com/about-us

Eli Whitney: Inventor of the Cotton Gin

Books   Huff, Regan A. *Eli Whitney: The Cotton Gin and American Manufacturing.* The Library of American Lives and Times. New York: PowerKids Press, 2004.

Yafa, Stephen. *Cotton: The Biography of a Revolutionary Fiber.* New York: Penguin, 2005.

Websites **How the Cotton Gin Changed America**
www.youtube.com/watch?v=bns6aKfrljA

Who Made America?: Eli Whitney
www.pbs.org/wgbh/theymadeamerica/whomade/whitney_hi.html

Index

Index